# Embroidered Books

# Embroidered Books

Isobel Hall

BATSFORD

# Acknowledgements

My thanks go to all my friends and the suppliers who have helped and encouraged me and to Pfaff for the loan of the needle-felting Embellisher machine.

As always my husband has been my rock and I thank him for putting me first and devoting his well-earned retirement to me.

First published in the United Kingdom in 2009 by
Batsford
10 Southcombe Street
London
W14 0RA

An imprint of Anova Books Company Ltd

ISBN 978 1 9063 8813 3

A CIP catalogue record for this book is available from the British Library.

17 16 15 14 13 12 11 10 09
10 9 8 7 6 5 4 3 2 1

Reproduction by Craft Print Ltd, Singapore
Printed and bound by Rival Colour Ltd, UK

This book can be ordered direct from the publisher at the website www.anovabooks.com, or try your local bookshop.

Distributed in the United States and Canada by
Sterling Publishing Co., 387 Park Avenue South, New York, NY 10016, USA

# Contents

# Introduction

Handmade books are lovely things to own and receive and there are many ways of decorating the books once you have made them. In this book I will show you how to construct books and how to work with mixed-media techniques and stitch to individualize both the covers and the inside pages.

The emphasis throughout this book has been on working with modern-day materials that are robust, durable and suitable for embroidery. I have tried to keep the pages of the books a manageable size, so that many of them could be suitable for use as address books, notebooks, sketchbooks and postcard albums. The wedding books featured on page 14 are very popular for use at wedding receptions for guests to write notes and comments for the bride and groom. In addition to these useable books, I have also included one or two decorated art books, which stand as works of art in their own right, and readable storybooks.

When working with the techniques explained in the book, an experimental approach will result in unique artwork, which could also be applicable for other three-dimensional work, wall art and sketchbook work. I hope that once you have mastered the art of bookmaking you will go on to explore using these mixed-media techniques for your own individual artwork. A useful rule of thumb is that when you are working with mixed media you should keep evaluating your work as you go, and stop adding materials once you are happy with the results on your fabric.

I hope you get as much enjoyment as I do from creating and using your embroidered books.

Left: This book cover features a collage flower embroidered in long-leg cross stitch, outlined in puff paint. Instructions for constructing a book like this are given overleaf.
Right: Medieval trebuchet book stand. Cocoon-stripping books using different mixed-media techniques.

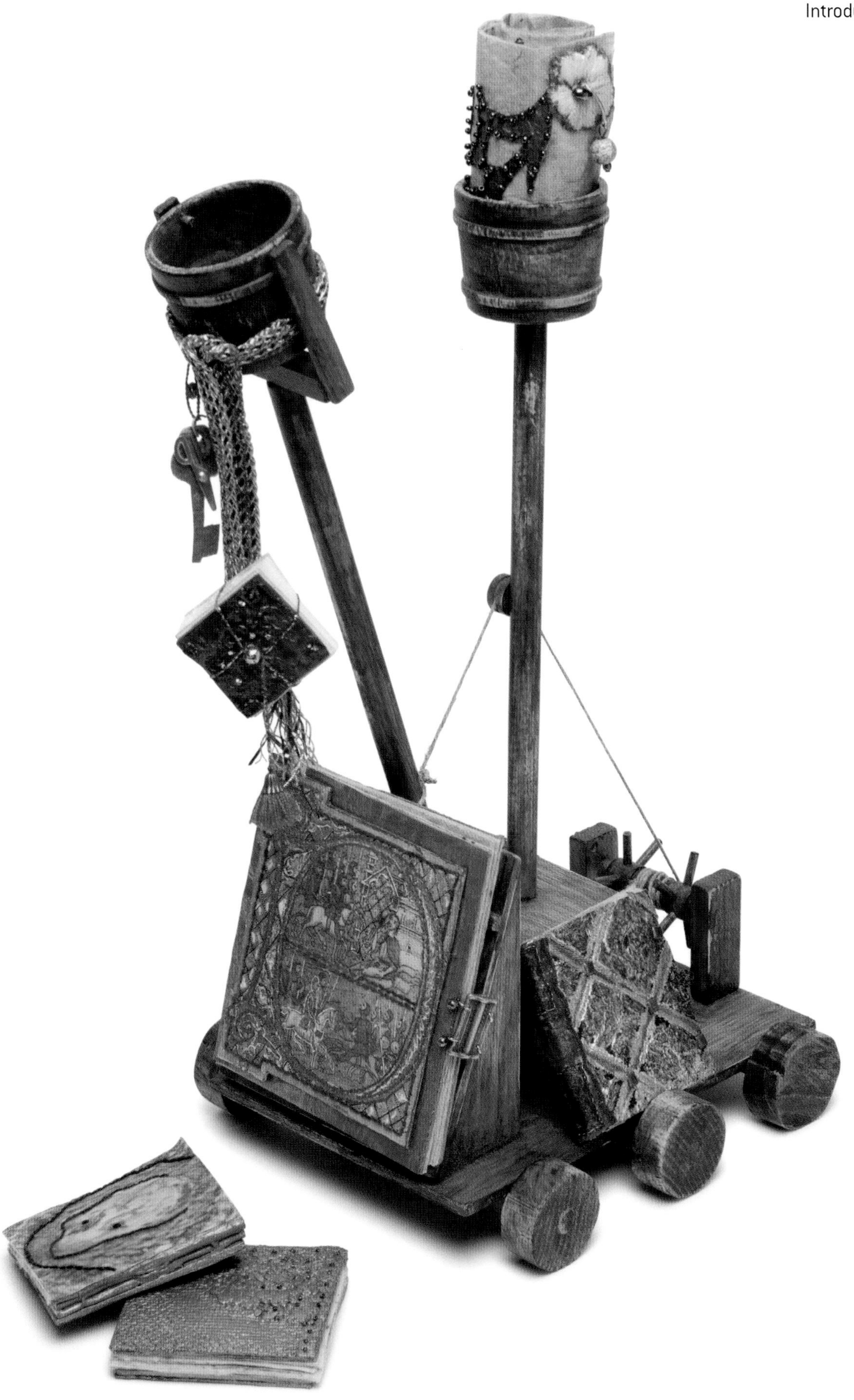

# 1. BOOK CONSTRUCTION

Fishing in Garrucha.
Fish recipe book with bonded
sheer fish, made by Xantha Hall.

# Books with embroidered spines

## Book sections, signatures or folios

A single page of a book is known as a folio. If two or three pages are placed inside each other these are called a signature or section. The pages can be made out of many different materials. Here are some suggestions:

- Thin **writing papers** make good books to write in. Because they are thin, they have a tendency to tear when the signatures are being sewn together. **Tip:** Pull the needle and thread straight when tightening the pages. If you pull the thread to one side the holes will tear.
- **Sugar paper** is heavier and cheaper. It is not acid-free and the colours do fade. It is suitable for simple books bound with Japanese-style bindings as it is easy to stitch into. However, for this style of book I prefer **mulberry paper**. Alternatively, the cheaper and less tactile **Khadi papers** can be used.
- For books with open embroidered spines, **card** is more versatile as its strength will hold embroidery samples within the book. These can be positioned with glue and if it is used sparingly the card should not buckle.
- Other materials to consider are pages made from **silk papers** and **pulp paper**. The latter is more time-consuming but recycled papers do not cost anything. Pulp papers will not be as strong as silk paper and will tear. Silk paper does not fray and will remain robust.
- Bought **fabrics that do not fray** can also be used. These can be decorated prior to assembly. The lightweight craft Vilene (Pellon) used throughout this book is firm and stable and not as thick as the heavy-duty pelmet Vilene, which some traders refer to as craft Vilene. It is worth searching for this lighter variety as it is much more versatile for book-making.
- Bought or hand-woven **fabrics that do fray** need consideration. Sometimes frayed edges are desirable so this is not a problem. Generally speaking they should be worked on prior to assembly.

## Cutting and folding the paper

Robust paper trimmers are the best option. Other options, apart from scissors, are a craft knife or rotary cutter used on a self-healing mat. Craft knives work well on grey board but tend to tear papers.

Most but not all of the books in this book require a folded page. The fold should ideally be made so that it lies parallel to the grain in the paper. Keeping the grain in the same direction eliminates curled or buckled pages. It is worth investing in a bone folder as they help to produce crisp, clean folds.

# Preparing the sections or signatures

1   Fold and cut your pile of papers to size, keeping the grain in the same direction. Check to see that the sizes are correct. If three pages or folios are placed inside each other to make signatures, the edges may require further trimming. A lot depends upon the thickness of the paper.

2   **Making a template:** Accurate positioning of the holes is crucial as the paper will tear when you are sewing it up if you do not have the holes aligned correctly. A template that can be placed over the valley folds of the signatures or folios is therefore necessary. You need to work out how many tapes you would like to use (two are used in the drawing shown below) and also consider how wide your tape is. The two end holes should be positioned 1cm (½in) in from the edge. Use a ruler to work out the spaces between the holes so that they are equally spaced.

3   The template shown below was made from a folded piece of card. It shows the two end holes and the position for two tapes (six holes in total). These were measured and marked in pencil prior to being pierced. The holes can be made by piercing the card with a sharp needle.

4   Once the template has been made you need to pierce holes in all of the folios or signatures. Line up the template with the first folio or place the template in either each valley fold or mountain fold and use a sharp needle to pierce the holes in an accurate position. The holes should all be on the fold line and not slightly off. When all of the pages have been pierced they are ready to be sewn into a book block.

5   **Endpapers:** Cut and fold two endpapers. For beginners it is easier to make the cover, backing boards, endpapers and folios the same size. The endpapers can be made of card, marbled papers or papers of your choice. Use the template to pierce holes in the endpapers.

6   Place one endpaper at the front of the pile of signatures and one at the back. These will eventually be glued to the front and back backing boards to fasten the book block to the front and back covers.

7   **Thread:** Measure the length of thread needed to sew up the book pages. I usually wrap the thread around the template, counting the number of pages as I wrap. Add 25cm (10in) to this. Cut the thread. Beginners should not attempt to work with a long length of thread as it is easy to get it tangled. Keep the number of pages small until you have mastered the sewing process. As the thread is intended to show, select one that is appealing. Some threads will snag, shred or break so it is usually best to avoid these. Fine variegated silk has been used for most of the work illustrated throughout this book. Run the thread over a wax block or Thread Heaven to help prevent it from tangling.

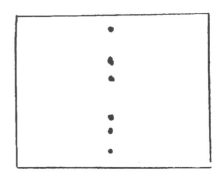

A basic page template.

## Tapes

Pulling the tapes tight and bonding them to the endpapers helps to tighten the book block. If the spine is intended to be exposed and the tapes are to be left in place, then careful consideration in selecting the tapes will add to the character of the book.

Tapes can be made from all manner of things. Traditionally tapes used by bookbinders are linen. These are robust and have the added advantage that the ends can be frayed and kept as a decorative feature or frayed and bonded to the endpapers of the book block. Any tape or fabric used should be strong enough to be pulled tight and it should not be bulky. Thick tapes will make the pages of the book slack.

Consider using ribbons, painted Lutradur strips, silk paper or other materials that do not fray for tapes. Books can be made unique by individualizing the tapes. The width of the tape is also important when planning the decoration of a book with an open embroidered spine. Varying the size can sometimes be advantageous. Try wrapping different-sized tapes around the folios to help you to select the right one.

Tapes can be pulled and used on the front and back covers as added decoration, or they can be pulled out and removed altogether. The tapes were removed from the Chatelaine's Girdle book illustrated below. The embroidery on the spine resembles smocking because thin thread was used and also because it is a small, fat book with many folios.

Chatelaine's Girdle.
Spine with smocking.

# Sewing the book block

### Purpose-built spine-sewing frames

People work in various ways when assembling book blocks. My preferred choice is to work with a purpose-built spine-sewing frame as illustrated below right (a). I like the versatility of these frames as they are not only stable but portable. I have got used to using these as they are easy to lift and work on at an angle if desired. However, if you do not have one, there are alternatives.

### Constructing a home-made frame

A simple frame can be contrived by using an interlocking embroidery sewing frame and a pile of table mats.

### You will need:

- a rectangular embroidery sewing frame wide enough to accommodate the book sections
- drawing pins (optional)
- masking tape
- at least two tapes long enough to stretch from the top of the frame and under the table
- three or four table mats
- pencil
- ruler

a

1   Measure the distance required between the tapes.

2   Use drawing pins to attach the tapes in this required position to the top of the frame (see b, right). Or use masking tape to secure the tapes. I prefer masking tape as it is easy to reposition the tapes should it become necessary.

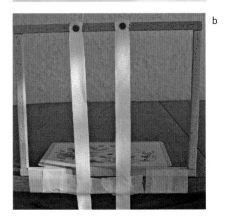
b

3   Use masking tape to secure the sewing frame and the bottom of the tapes to the edge of the table.

4   You will need a flat base to work on which is the same height as the bottom of the sewing frame. I use three table mats piled up to achieve this. As you want a firm base with little or no movement, these need to be attached to the bottom bar of the sewing frame with masking tape. The home-made sewing frame is now ready to be used.

If you have an appropriate dining chair it could be used as an alternative spine-sewing frame. Attach the tapes to the top of the chair with masking tape. Attach the bottom of the tapes to the underneath of the chair back. Place the signatures one at a time on the flat bed of the chair with the fold at the back of the chair. Work with the chair back facing you.

c

Here are some instructions for sewing the book block:

1    Thread a sharp needle with the thread of your choice.

2    Check that the holes on the fold line of the endpaper are in line with the tapes, and place one of the endpapers on the flat bed of the sewing frame. Sit with the tapes facing you and the endpaper at the other side.

3    Note where the first hole is on the right and insert the needle into this hole, thus pulling the thread to the inside (valley) fold of the endpaper. Use masking tape to secure the end of the sewing thread to the underside of the frame in line with the first hole. Always pull the thread straight to tighten each hole. If you pull it at an angle the paper will tear.

4    Insert the needle through the second hole in the endpaper and pull the thread through. A stitch now runs along the inside fold of the paper and the thread comes out on the mountain side of the fold next to the first tape. Take care not to catch the tape with the needle.

5    Pass the thread around the tape and through the next hole in the endpaper, again making sure you don't stitch through the tape. Continue to stitch to the end. Pull each stitch as tightly as you can without tearing the paper. Your thread should run in front of each tape and finally emerge at the left-hand side.

6    Place the first signature or folio on top of the endpaper. Check that the holes are aligned in the correct position. Take the needle through the first hole on the left-hand side. Bring it back out through the next hole, adjacent to the tape. As before, remember to pull each stitch tightly. Slide the needle up through the thread that is visible going over that tape. (It is essential to remember to do this each time you come to a tape as it makes the book block stronger and is a decorative feature. Go under and up the thread on the left-hand side each time you come to a tape to help maintain a good stitch pattern.) Continue sewing across to the right-hand side, where the thread should emerge at the front (see the diagram on page 14).

7    Undo the starting thread, which is attached to the base with masking tape. Tie this end to the sewing thread so that it is secure. Use masking tape to pull the starting thread out of the way again and hold it in position under the sewing frame with the tape.

8    Take the second signature and place it on top of the pile on the flat bed of the sewing frame. Check that the holes are in line.

9    Take the needle in through the first (right-hand) hole and out through the second hole. You will be at the first tape. Bring the needle up through the thread going over the tape and keep to the right-hand side of the previous stitch on the lower signature. Continue until you reach the end.

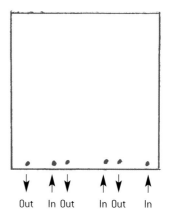

Above: Stitching in and out of the prepared holes in the book block.
Opposite page: a) A purpose-built spine-sewing frame; b) A home-made version; c) A finished sewn book block on a frame.

**10** When you are at the end you will be working on the left-hand side of the block and will have come out of the end hole. Slide the needle through the loop connecting the lower signatures. You need to do this each time you come to the end. This tightens the book block. If you forget to do it at either end it will result in a floppy book.

**12** Continue placing one signature at a time on the book block and sew in the same manner, remembering to catch the stitch going over the tapes each time and also the loop at each end, as shown in the diagram below.

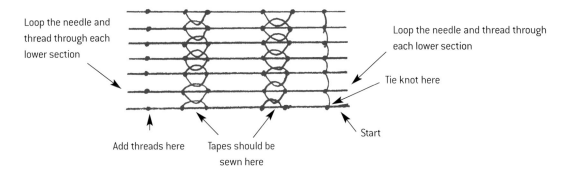

Loop the needle and thread through each lower section

Loop the needle and thread through each lower section

Tie knot here

Start

Add threads here

Tapes should be sewn here

**13** The last folio to be stitched will be the second endpaper. Sew this in position and remember to slip the thread through the bottom loop connecting the lower signatures.

**14** Remove the masking tape and lift the book block off the frame.

**15** Use masking tape to secure the ends of the thread to the back of the endpapers.

**16** Trim the tapes, leaving sufficient tape to bond them to the endpapers. Use masking tape to do this. The front and back endpapers will eventually be bonded to the front and back backing boards.

Wedding books with heavily beaded open embroidered spines. To bead the spine, add the beads to the threads when you reach each tape position.

# Backing boards

The front and back backing boards are essential to give the book rigidity. You can buy boards from specialist dealers or you can use heavy grey board, available from paper and art suppliers. The boards which you can buy from specialist dealers are usually referred to as mill board or binder's board; they are thicker than grey board and are therefore difficult to cut. Most of the books with open embroidered spines illustrated in this book have grey board backing boards as these can be cut using a craft knife on a cutting board.

Boards that are going to be stitched into could be made from pelmet Vilene (Pellon) or buckram. Thick pulp papers make good backing boards, especially if you want them to be stitched into. Another alternative could be to use wadding. This, of course, would not be as rigid but it would be more tactile. If a rigid backing board is required you could bond your cover to wadding, stitch into it and then bond the wadding to grey board.

# Endpapers

The endpapers for books with rigid spines could be marbled papers, bought silk papers or specially designed papers of your choice. As one side will be glued to the backing board it is important that it fits the board exactly, unless the cover on the backing board is wrapped around the backing board. Covers that wrap around the backing board make for a more professional-looking book but the fabric needs to be thin enough for you to be able to mitre the corners. The cheapest glue to use to bond the endpapers to the backing boards is PVA (white craft glue). Use it sparingly to prevent buckled pages and do not use it on porous surfaces, as it could seep through and spoil the cover. Insert a sheet of baking parchment between the front and back pages to prevent excess glue going where you do not want it. Place a heavy weight on the completed book to keep it flat during the drying process.

Ashness Bridge. Cocoon-stripping folios with an open embroidered spine.

# PROJECT
# Enamelled book covers

There are many different varieties of embossing powders that can be used for book covers. I have tried most of them, and certain ones become favourites – ones that are easy to stitch into without cracking or crumbling. The following project uses a distress powder in conjunction with an embossing enamel.

**You will need:**
- craft knife, cutting board and metal ruler
- sandpaper
- grey board
- mulberry paper or bookbinder's tissue
- heat-fixable paint such as Stewart Gill Byzantia
- peeled-paint distress embossing powder
- heat gun
- Opals embossing enamels
- cotton quilter's wadding or lightweight Vilene (Pellon)
- 505 spray glue
- PVA glue (white craft glue)
- threads for embroidering the paper
- papers for the folios or signatures
- three tapes
- endpapers

1　Cut the boards to size. A craft knife or Stanley knife is usually necessary for this. Use a metal ruler to cut against.

2　Use sandpaper to smooth the edges and to round the corners, if desired. Rounded corners are usually best if the covers are wrapped around the backing board. If the covers are flush to the backing board and endpapers the corners should not be rounded (as in my example).

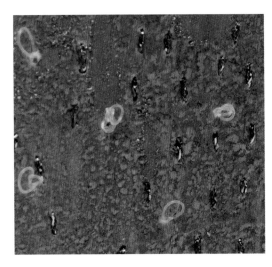

Detail of the front of the book.

3　Decorate the paper covers. The covers for the book opposite were made from bookbinder's tissue. The tissue was painted with Stewart Gill Byzantia heat-fixable paint. While it was still wet, peeled-paint distress embossing powder was sprinkled on. The crystals were melted with a heat gun. (Note: If embossing powders blow away when heat is applied it means that they are not stuck to the paint, which usually means that another, thicker coat of paint should be applied.) While the distress powders were still hot, Opals embossing enamels were sprinkled on in selected areas and heated with a heat gun.

4　Bond the paper to cotton quilter's wadding using 505 spray glue, then stitch and embroider the paper. I used fishing wire and thick yarn for the project shown (see detail, right).

5    Use PVA to bond the grey backing boards to the front and back covers.

6    Cut the folios or signatures the same size as the backing boards.

7    Select the tapes of your choice and sew the book block (see pages 12–14), adding beads if desired. If you add beads, slide them onto the thread when you reach each tape.

8    Use PVA glue (white craft glue) to bond the endpapers to the front and back grey backing boards. Use the PVA sparingly as overuse will result in buckled pages.

9    Place a heavy weight on the book until the glue is completely dry.

The enamelled covers on this book were embroidered for added decoration. The spine was beaded and the tags made from bonded sheers.

# PROJECT
# Wrap-up books

These books are fun to make, use and hold. They are quite compact and can be made to any size. This book cover is made from silk paper but any fabric that does not fray is suitable. The backing boards for this wrap-up book are the same size as the paper used for the signatures.

This wrap-up book measures 11 x 11cm ($4^{1}/_{2}$ x $4^{1}/_{2}$in).

**You will need:**
- sufficient silk paper or non-fray fabric to embroider two squares, 11 x 11cm (4½ x 4½in)
- craft knife, cutting board and metal ruler
- 11cm (4½in) square thick card or grey board
- thin cord to match
- matching variegated cotton
- 2 large buttons
- PVA (white craft glue)
- spatula or old paintbrush to apply the glue
- 2 tapes
- sharp needle
- paper or card for the signatures
- paper for endpapers

1   Cut the grey board to size.

2   Embroider your chosen non-fray fabric.

3   Cut the fabric to the exact size.

4   Sparingly use PVA to bond the fabric to the front and back backing boards. (Too much PVA will seep through the silk paper and be unsightly.)

5   Cut the paper signatures to the exact size.

6   Sew the signatures in place, as explained on pages 12–14.

7   Attach one end of the wrapping cord to the centre-front backing board. (Alternatively, the cord could be attached to the button with a loop as shown.)

8   Attach the buttons to the centre front and back of the backing boards.

The wrap-up book closed.

**9** Use PVA to bond the front backing board to the front endpaper and the back backing board to the back endpaper. (To protect the other papers it is a good idea to place a large sheet of baking parchment between the pages in case any glue goes where it is unwanted.)

**10** Leave this to dry before opening the book.

To personalize your books you could try making the button yourself. Try Softsculpt, Mylar, embossing enamels on metal buttons or glue-gun patches. Anything you use must be robust enough for the purpose.

Tassels could become a major feature on these wrap-up books.

Wrap-up book open, showing the exposed embroidered spine.

# PROJECT
# Porcelain tile-effect covers

Pulp papers can be made to resemble ceramic tiles. Any tough sealer can be used for this technique, but I prefer the one made by Jo Sonja's (see Suppliers, page 126) as it gives an extremely hardy, ceramic-like finish.

**You will need:**
- fibres to be trapped
- pulp paper or Lokta pulp paper
- PVA (white craft glue) diluted with water
- paints of your choice, such as Brusho, silk paints or Procion dyes
- needle and threads of your choice
- encaustic wax and iron
- Jo Sonja's All Purpose Sealer
- grey board
- card or paper of your choice for the pages
- Metal spring-loaded ring binders
- hole punch
- **Optional:** lightweight Vilene (Pellon) or quilter's wadding; peeled-paint embossing powders and heat-fixable paint for the edges.

1  To create the covers:
- Trap fibres in a grid formation in pulp paper. Alternatively, you can use Lokta paper. Wet the Lokta paper and push the fibres into position. Paint with diluted PVA, if desired.
- Colour the paper when it is dry or it will be very porous. Use thin paint such as Brusho, silk dyes or Procion dyes. The paper opposite was not coloured as it was pale turquoise when the pulp paper was made.
- If the paper is rather flimsy it should be backed onto lightweight Vilene or quilter's wadding. This paper was robust so could be stretched in an embroidery frame. (Note: If you stretch the paper in a frame the pins will leave marks, so allow sufficient paper to cut it down in size afterwards.)
- Melt encaustic wax on an encaustic iron or travel iron that does not have steam vents. Iron the melted wax over the raised surfaces on the paper.
- Embroider the paper.
- Paint Jo Sonja's sealer at full strength over the paper. This will change the appearance of the paper and the stitches. The surface of the paper will become extremely hard and it is this sealer which makes the paper resemble porcelain. (If you do not want a tough sealer, the paper can be left as it is or painted with acrylic wax or diluted PVA.)
- Bond the paper to grey board using the diluted PVA.
- Paint the edges. (**Optional:** Add peeled-paint embossing powders to the edges and heat with a heat gun. You need to use heat-fixable paint if you intend to do this.)
2  Cut your paper or card pages to size. No fold is necessary for this technique.

3   Make a card template for the holes. Use a ruler and pencil to mark the position for these and use a hole punch to punch the holes in the template.

4   Place the template over the paper or card to be used for the pages. Hold it in position with a bulldog clip.

5   Punch the holes in the papers. You may have to do one at a time if your hole punch will not take more. You may also have to keep removing the small circles of paper if they get trapped in the hole punch. Alternatively a Japanese screw punch could be used. These are easier to use but they are more costly.

6   Punch holes in the covers and thread the metal spring ring binders in position to finish.

Porcelain-effect covers that have been dyed,
waxed, embroidered and sealed.

# Post screws

Books made with post screws are useful if you are going to want to remove and add pages at a later date.

The important thing to remember when making books of this type is that when you want to turn the pages over you must be able to turn the front cover easily. In order to do this it is necessary to have a fold near the post screws. There are a few ways in which you could do this.

- Use heavy pelmet Vilene (Pellon) or buckram as it is possible to obtain a fold line on these.
- Use a thinner grey board or card which will bend and fold without cracking (I used this for the Sarlat Geese book shown opposite).
- Another way is to use two pieces of heavier grey board and leave a gap between them (see the diagram below). They can be hinged together with masking tape or they can be bonded to the back of the cover if the fabric is robust (this was used for the Driftwood book shown opposite).

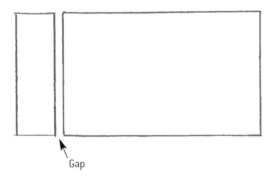

Gap

Pages made for these books are made from one single sheet with no fold lines. The holes are punched through each paper and through the back and front covers. If the post screws are too long for the thickness of the book this can be rectified by adding washers. The washers could be covered with buttonhole stitch and strings of beads or other items could be added. Alternatively, narrow strips of card could be cut and inserted between the pages to act as spacers.

Sarlat Geese and Driftwood. These covers are made from pulp paper formed from tissue papers, autumn leaves and cotton linters. The pages are secured in place with post screws.

# Japanese-style bindings

These books are quite crudely made, but the simplicity of their style can be very effective.

- Begin by making the front and back covers. The front cover needs to be pliable so that it can be turned back to open the book.
- Next, cut a pile of papers to size. No fold is necessary for this technique.
- Measure and mark the sewing holes. For the purple book opposite seven holes were equally spaced. (Five or seven holes are usually sufficient.) Mark these holes lightly in pencil on the first page and use this as your template.
- Place the template over the pages and clip them together with a large bulldog clip to hold them in place.
- Use an awl or a needle with a large eye to pierce the marked holes in all of the pages and the covers.
- Place the covers in position and hold them in place with bulldog clips. If a binding tape is to be used, bond it around the edges using PVA (white craft glue). I did this for the large book shown opposite.
- Use your chosen thread to sew the book together. Strong thread or ribbon is advisable.
- From the back come up through the first hole (point 1). Leave thread hanging at the back as you will need it to tie a knot when all the sewing is finished.
- Wrap the thread around the spine and come back through the same hole again so that the thread is at the front (point 1).
- Take the thread down to the next hole (point 2) and stitch through it so that the thread is on the back cover (point 2).
- Wrap the thread around the spine and go through the same hole so that the thread still lies on the back cover (point 2).
- Take the thread to the next hole (point 3) and bring the thread up through it.
- Wrap the thread around the spine and come up through the same hole (point 3).
- Continue down the spine in this way until you reach point 7. The thread will be on the front cover. Take the thread and wrap it around the bottom of the book and come through the hole at point 7.
- Continue sewing back up using running stitch to fill in the gaps.
- When you reach the top, take the thread through point 1 and wrap it around the top edge of the book.
- Tie the two threads together at the back and pull the knot tight.

The larger book has Japanese-style binding over bamboo tape, while the smaller book has simple stab-stitch binding.

# Concertina-style books

## Needle-felted garden wall book

Studies of garden walls have been an ongoing project for me for a number of years, and I think they work especially well in this format. I created this book by first making sheets of thin, lacy silk paper, which were then felted and embroidered before being joined together.

Six pages should be made and embroidered separately prior to assembly. The pages are then placed with their insides together and connecting strips are sewn into the sides when the pages are sewn around the edges. (Silk carrier rods were used here.)

**Note:** the sides could have been bonded together by using the Embellisher machine but this was undesirable for this project as I did not want any further felting to occur.

- Begin by making sheets of silk paper. For the wall, silk throwster's waste and rayon fibres were bonded separately to make the thin, lacy paper. Acrylic gloss medium is my preferred choice for this technique. Protect the work surface with polythene sheeting. Spread net fabric on the work surface, tease the fibres and lay them on the net. Cover with another layer of net. Wet the fibres with a solution of water and washing-up liquid. Dilute the acrylic gloss medium with water. One teaspoon of acrylic gloss medium to four teaspoons of water makes a strong fabric. Paint this on the net and use the flat palms of your hands to push the glue into the fibres. Turn the layers over and repeat. Hang the layers of net up to dry. When they are dry, peel the netting off. Beige and stone-coloured papers were made to represent the wall. Green silk paper was made in the same way to represent the grass.
- Select wool or fibres of your choice. Red brick walls contain many colours and these need to be represented in the finished piece. Tease the fibres to make them fluffy.
- Ensure that you have sufficient paper for the grassed area underneath the wall as this will be worked on later. Place the two thin, lacy sheets of bonded papers together. Place some teased wool or silk fibres on top. Use an embellishing machine to bond the layers. Work in horizontal lines backwards and forwards, adding fibres as you go.
- The reverse side will be the side you will eventually be working on so keep turning the fabric over to look at it to see how it is progressing.
- Place a thin layer of white polyester wadding over the front of the work. Do not use the Embellisher machine for any further work.
- Place dyed green net over part of the wall. (I used dressmaker's net that had previously been used to make silk paper.)

Victorian Garden Wall concertina book.

- Cover the wall with brown sheer fabric. Voile was used here as it has a coarse texture compared to sheer organza, and it also knocked back the colour to a greater extent.
- Use variegated thread to make stitches to represent the wall. Experimentation led me to believe that uneven stitches, worked informally, looked better than a formal representation.
- Place black FuseFX webbing over the wall. Cover it with baking parchment. Iron briefly with a hot iron. Look to see if the webbing has bonded successfully. If you use a hot iron the webbing will melt quickly and change the appearance of the fabric. Prolonged use of heat may not be to your liking.
- Use 505 temporary adhesive spray to bond green silk paper over the bottom part or needle felt it in place.
- Embroider the flowers.
- Assemble the concertina-style book by laying the pages back to back in pairs with connecting strips in between to join them; stitch the layers together.

Left: Detail of the Victorian Garden Wall book,
showing the layers of paper, fibre and net and
some of the embroidery work.
Above: The back of the book.

# Flagpoles for concertina-style books

This free-standing book depicts the story of the Quest of the Holy Grail. It was made on blue craft Vilene (Pellon). Two strips of Vilene measuring 46 x 16cm (18 x 6in) were cut and then each panel was worked on separately. When the two sides were finished they were placed back to back and carefully sewn together.

   The flagpoles on which the book stands were made from wrapped sticks. The sticks stand in large wooden beads that have been painted and embossed with powders. The sticks are permanently and securely embedded in the beads with glue from a hot-melt glue gun. They are all capped by a painted, embroidered and beaded silk cocoon pod. The flags are made from Lutradur and they 'fly in the wind' as they have paper-wrapped wire sewn to the edges.

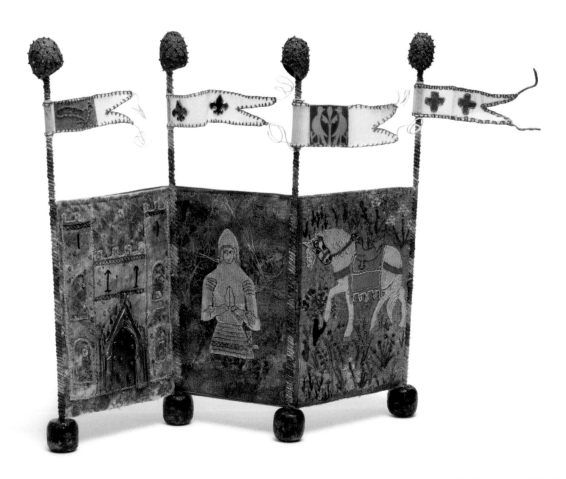

Above: The Quest for the Holy Grail.
Silk paper on blue craft Vilene.
Right: the other side of the book.

# Concertina-style books on card

This book can be read by standing it up in a zigzag formation or by looking at two pages at a time, as you would read a conventional book. The book shown below, which commemorates buildings seen on holidays, has lightweight Vilene (Pellon) pages that are bonded to card. A continuous length of card is therefore needed. A sheet of A3-sized card, which is cut to size and then folded at equally spaced intervals, forms the shape for the book. Valley folds alternate with mountain folds to achieve this effect. For the book shown, 14 images were needed. At each end there is a grey board backing board and these also need images on them. As so many images were needed and as I did not want the book to become fat and unwieldy I decided to use lightweight craft Vilene for the images inside the book (see page 64 for the techniques used on the interior pages).

- Decorate the pages for the accordion-style book block. I used the techniques described on page 64. Cut the card to size and carefully fold it into equally spaced sections.
- Cut grey board to size for the front and back covers.
- Use PVA (white craft glue) to bond the grey board to the first and last pages of the folded card.
- Use your artwork to cover the front and back covers and the pages. Use PVA sparingly as too much will result in buckled pages. Place a heavy weight on top while it is drying as this helps to reduce buckling. **Tip:** place sheets of baking parchment between the pages to eliminate the possibility of PVA going where you do not want it.

# Shaped books

## Vase-shaped books

Unusually shaped books are fun to make and can still be functional. The vase-shaped bowed book shown on page 34 was made from cocoon-stripping paper covers with card signatures. Normally you would ensure that the grain on the papers runs in the same direction (i.e. vertically). However, in this case you will need to ignore this rule and work with papers that have the grain running in diverse directions. Painting on these and not drying them flat will result in buckled, bowed pages. Do not paint them until the book is assembled as explained below.

   The front cover for this book is very solid and bowed due to many layers of PVA (white craft glue) between the endpaper, the grey board and the cocoon-stripping paper. Note that this book has two backing boards, one made from lightweight craft Vilene (Pellon) and then another made from grey board.

- Cut cocoon-stripping paper (see page 45) or mulberry paper to size. (Cocoon-stripping paper was used here.)
- Colour the paper with your chosen paints. Brusho, silk dyes, Twinkling H2Os, poster paints or acrylic paints are all suitable.
- When it is dry, paint acrylic wax over it and add gold flakes, if desired.
- When this is dry, rub beeswax furniture polish into the paper and buff it.
- If the finish is to your liking go to the next stage. Alternatively, paint a layer of varnish over the paper (clear nail varnish was used for this book cover).
- **Optional:** Protect your hands with rubber gloves and squeeze a few drops of Adirondack Alcohol Ink in Terra Cotta onto a piece of wadding. Apply this to the paper. It will change the colour of the paper and it will knock back the brightness of the gold flakes.
- Add artwork of your choice (I used a lion printed onto Jacquard Extravorganza in this instance).
- The book block for the vase-shaped book shown overleaf was assembled by stitching the signatures at the top of the vase. The tapes were left in place and painted brown.
- The backing boards for the book need consideration at this stage. Lightweight Vilene is porous and this was bonded to the cocoon-stripping paper prior to stitching. Cotton quilter's wadding is also porous and could be used as an alternative, if desired. Stitch into the cocoon-stripping paper and embroider it as desired.
- The following instructions should be carried out immediately and simultaneously as the distortion required is dependent upon the amount of glue used to bond the covers to the book block and the paint used to paint the pages of the signatures.

- Paint both sides of the signatures or folios. Card folios were used here. Do not place a weight on top as you want the card to curl. You may need to place baking parchment between the pages to prevent them from sticking together.
- Cut a piece of grey board to size. Use PVA to bond the grey board to the lightweight Vilene that backs the cocoon-stripping paper cover.
- Paint the edges with acrylic paint.
- Bond the grey board to the endpaper on the book block. Use a large amount of PVA.
- Repeat for the back backing board.

Vase-shaped book with covers
made from cocoon-stripping paper,
coloured, embellished and waxed.

Top: The closed heart-shaped book.
Above: The centre page of the heart-shaped book.
When it is opened, one heart becomes two.

# Carousel books

There are numerous ways in which to make this type of book. The example shown below was made on lightweight Vilene (Pellon) as it is easy to stitch into but remains rigid enough for the pages to stand without any extra support when it is opened as a carousel.

- Draw one double page on lightweight Vilene. The measurements for this book were 18cm (7in) high and 12cm (4¾in) wide and so each double page measured 18 x 24cm (7 x 9½in).
- Cut this out.
- Draw another double-sized page on the Vilene and cut it out.
- Work out how many pages there will be in the book. This book contains 14 images on the pages, plus the two covers.
- Work out on which pages to place your images as, when the book is assembled, they will not necessarily be opposite each other. Remember to leave one side of the page blank at the front and the back as these will be the endpapers which will eventually be glued to the covers.
- Create your artwork on the first sheet of Vilene. Each page should be coloured and the images stitched. You can work directly on the Vilene or you can work on other papers and then appliqué each panel to the Vilene page.
- Appliqué your artwork to the second sheet of Vilene or work directly on it, as before.
- Place the embroidered Vilene pages back to back with the insides together and sew around the edges. This can be done by machine or hand. The pages of this book were sewn by hand in running stitch to give it a rustic feel. Go all the way around all four sides in running stitch and then continue around so that it resembles backstitch on both sides of the pages. Start with a knot which is concealed between the two sheets and finish by sliding the needle with the thread through an inconspicuous space and thus avoid double stitches.
- When all of the pages have been worked on they are ready to be assembled as a book with an open embroidered spine (see page 9).
- Place the pages in a pile and check that you have two endpapers to glue to the backing boards.
- Sew the pages as if you were creating a book with an embroidered spine. (The fold line will be fat but easy to stitch into.)
- Decide whether to remove the tapes or leave them in place. (Try pulling the end pages together to help you to decide. Sometimes it is an advantage to pull the tapes really tight.) In this instance the tapes were removed.
- Create your artwork on the fabric or paper of your choice for the front and back covers.

The opened carousel book.

- Glue the artwork to the backing boards. Do not use thick grey board as this will inhibit the carousel movement.
- Insert cord or ribbon between the backing board and the endpapers and use PVA to bond the backing boards to the endpapers.

The closed carousel book.

# Waterfall pages

These can be inserted on a page in a book as part of the book or they can be made as a book in itself, as can be seen in the Sing a Song of Sixpence waterfall book opposite. These work by having a tab that can be pulled so that a series of pictures turn and one image after another is revealed. In this example the 'slide show' reveals images from the nursery rhyme 'Sing a Song of Sixpence'. When the tab has been pulled to its extreme and it is pushed back, the pages turn and lie in position again. As these are intended to have constant use they must be robust enough to withstand the pulling and pushing of the tab mechanism. Lightweight Vilene (Pellon) is very good for this as it can be coloured, covered if desired, and stitched into; it doesn't fray and will remain strong enough to endure these actions.

Waterfall actions can be made to flow in either a vertical or horizontal direction. To obtain the best effect the front and the back images on each revolving page should contain the same image (see pages 40–41).

Five images, which are all the same size, should be prepared and duplicated so that you have ten images in total. As there will be a back and a front there will only be five pages with the same image on each side.

The back and front of each image should be made separately on a lightweight Vilene base. When both of these sides have been embroidered they can be bonded with the insides together and stitched around the edges. Lightweight Vilene is recommended as each page should not be too thick. Thick pages will inhibit the revolving mechanism.

The pulling tab should be the same width as the revolving pages but it must be long enough to be folded over and bend around the back (see instructions for the waterfall page for 'The Highwayman' on page 40). When the book is closed the tab will lie directly under the pile of pages. When the tab is pulled it will be extended and reveal any images that are otherwise hidden. It is therefore a good idea to consider this and embroider an appropriate image on the end of the tab. The tab made for this book reveals the king's crown. It is also made on lightweight Vilene. The background for the book was made from Pelmet Vilene that was covered in robust silk paper.

Sing a Song of Sixpence. Waterfall book on a leather-effect silk paper background. Pull the tab to activate the waterfall action. As the tag is pulled and the pages turn, the king's crown is revealed on the pulling tag.

4 and 20 blackbirds baked in a pie

The images below demonstrate the waterfall action that was made to illustrate part of the story in the Highwayman book. The book itself is a large, robust one, with embroidered pages appliquéd to card folios. This scene depicts the soldiers marching in the sunset. The tab is pulled in a horizontal position and the soldiers march across the page. As the images are all the same, this works better when the tab is pulled quickly.

The sunset was printed onto silk paper and this was bonded to lightweight Vilene (Pellon). The Vilene was in turn eventually bonded to the card page after the mechanism was assembled.

5 x 25cm (2 x 10in)

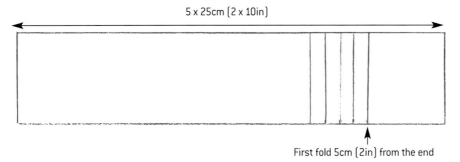

First fold 5cm (2in) from the end

- Ten equally sized squares of Vilene, 5 x 5cm (2 x 2in) need to be cut out (five fronts and five backs). In order to integrate the waterfall pages more successfully into the background picture on these two pages, I printed the sunset design onto A4 sheets of lightweight Vilene and cut them out.
- Five of the squares designated for the front can then be decorated, with one soldier embroidered on each of the five squares.
- The remaining five squares can either be decorated with the same images or left blank.
- Place the squares together in pairs with the insides together and sew around the edges with invisible thread.
- Cut two strips of Vilene 5 x 25cm (2 x 10in). The strips used for this mechanism were cut from Vilene which had the background image printed on it.

- One of the strips can be embroidered where the pulling tag will be (the left-hand side of the diagram but on the back). **Tip:** try assembling the strip before you embroider so that you embroider in the correct position.
- Put the wrong sides together and use invisible thread to sew the two strips together. (Consider bonding them with 505 prior to stitching as this will ensure a stronger tab.)
- Fold the strip as shown in the diagram. The first fold will be 5cm (2in) in from the right. The next four folds will be 1cm (⅜in) apart.
- Use double-sided tape to fasten one of the embroidered squares to the square on the right-hand side of the long Vilene strip.
- Use double-sided tape to place a bonding strip down the four remaining spaces between the folds.
- Attach each embroidered square to the tape so that they are in a staggered formation.
- Fold the Vilene under immediately after the last one has been attached.
- Prepare the background. The backgrounds for this page and the Sing a Song of Sixpence book were made on lightweight Vilene, covered with silk paper.
- For the next stage it is necessary to cut two slits through the silk paper and the Vilene on the background page. Accurate positioning is essential. I lined the group of marching soldiers up and measured carefully before making the slits. The finished page measures 22 x 18cm (9 x 7in). The first slit was 7cm (2½in) from the right. The second slit was 2cm (¾in) away. A craft knife was used to cut the slits, which should be the height of the pulling tab, i.e. 5cm (2in).
- Double-sided tape was placed between the two slits and the top of the tape was left covered.
- The long end of the soldier strip was threaded through this slit.
- When it was lined up, the tape covering the bottom strip was removed and the last square with a soldier on it was fastened to this. PVA (white craft glue) could be used for a more permanent bonding but it is wise to use double-sided tape in the first instance to ensure correct alignment.

Far left and left: the waterfall pages, showing soldiers in the Highwayman book, in action. Other pages from this book are shown on pages 62, 63 and 67.

# Box books

This box book opens out to lie flat and has triangular pages. The construction of these boxes is very simple and it is easy to adapt the sizes as the basic shape consists of a rectangle. As this box is made from lightweight Vilene (Pellon) it is quite sturdy. The triangular sides are made from copper relief foil, which is appliquéd to the Vilene base but, of course, this is optional.

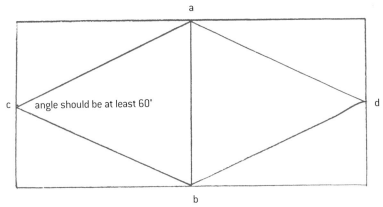

**Method**

- Draw a rectangle. The one for this book measured 30 x 10cm (12 x 4in).
- Measure and draw a line to mark the centre. (a–b)
- Draw a line from the centre of the side to point a. (c–a)
- Draw a line from c to b.
- Draw a line from d to point a.
- draw a line from d to b.
- Cut the large rectangle out.

Above: The box book closed.

Below: The box book opened out, lying flat.

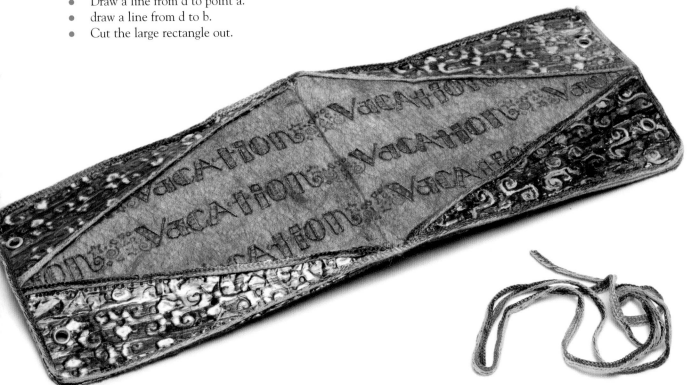

- Fold line a–c.
- Fold line a–d.
- Fold line c–b.
- Fold line d–b.
- When you have cut out your basic shape as described opposite you will see that the side flaps tuck inside each other to form a simple box construction. Fold these in prior to working out your design for the box.
- Colour or cover the Lightweight Vilene with artwork of your choice. The back and front should be covered. (Do not make it so thick that the eyelets will not go through.)
- Cut out triangular-shaped pages to fit in the box book as shown in the sample below.
- Decorate and stitch both sides of the pages. Two pieces per page are needed. Work on each side and then place them insides together and sew around the edges.
- Attach the completed triangular-shaped pages to the box book by placing them in the centre of the opened-out book. Machine stitch down the fold line using large stitches and invisible thread.
- Use an eyelet tool to punch eyelets in the four corners.
- Use ribbon or cord to tie the book, threading it through the eyelets.

The centre pages of the box book.

# 2. TECHNIQUES AND MATERIALS

All Things Medieval. Cocoon-stripping
paper book with Mylar spine and studs.

# Using cocoon strippings

Gummed cocoon strippings are easy to use and make excellent covers and pages. They only require water to bond the fibres but you will find that although the resulting paper looks robust, it will rapidly deteriorate when used. It does, therefore, need strengthening. You can do this in a number of ways, as described below. You will need to assemble gummed cocoon strippings, water in a spray bottle, baking parchment on the ironing board and a household iron.

- Tease the cocoon strippings and place a thin, lacy layer on the baking parchment. If you make the layer too thick, the fibres will not bond and you will end up with a fluffy patch, which will remain fragile. It is better to make very thin layers and build the paper up slowly.
- Spray the strippings with water.
- Cover with a second sheet of baking parchment.
- Iron with a household iron set on high. Cheap irons do not get hot enough to use for this technique.
- Remove the baking parchment and, working on top of the first layer of strippings, repeat until all the bare patches have been filled in. If you add to the size of the paper by laying down teased fibres around the edges, you will not leave a joining mark; the fibres will fuse together. Remember to spray water onto each layer. If you use too much water it will not matter, but you will have to keep the heat of the iron on the paper until it is dry.
- Strengthen the paper by painting a watered-down PVA (white craft glue) solution on top. Alternatively, you could use acrylic wax or Ormoline. Painting with one of these substances will seal the paper as well as strengthen it: cocoon paper is very porous until you do this. PVA will make the paper stiff and if you use too much it will be difficult to stitch into. Ormoline will leave a matt finish, while acrylic wax will be shiny. Ormoline and acrylic wax remain easy to stitch into.

### Ageing the papers
- To obtain aged papers, try ironing gold encaustic wax on the baking parchment prior to making the paper. Traces of the wax will be transferred to the cocoon-stripping paper when you work on top of this waxed baking parchment.
- Paint diluted coffee over the pages and iron dry under baking parchment.
- Try ironing black FuseFX webbing over the baking parchment. Place the cocoon-stripping paper over it. Cover with a second sheet of baking parchment and iron again. A whole piece of FuseFX does not look good so it is better to try to iron skimpy patches on the cocoon-stripping paper. If you have used FuseFX on another project and some residue remains on the baking parchment this is good to use over the cocoon-stripping paper.

# Cocoon strippings with gummy silk fibres

Gummy silk fibres and cocoon strippings can be bonded together by spraying water and applying the heat from a household iron. These should also be strengthened, as described on page 45.

Hard-backed book with a flap. Gummy silk and cocoon-stripping paper, with TLS flowers (see page 86).

This sketchbook's cover is paper made using silk fibres and kozo bark.

# Kozo bark

Silk fibres and kozo bark were bonded together to make the paper covers for the book shown above. The cover was made to represent the robes worn by Saint Francis of Assisi. The book itself was made as part of a study on Assisi and the cocoon-stripping pages hold sketchbook work based on this study. The tab fastens with a magnetic fastener.

# Wallet-style books with fabric pages

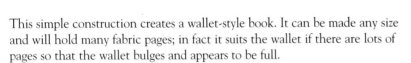

Flap

Fold line

This simple construction creates a wallet-style book. It can be made any size and will hold many fabric pages; in fact it suits the wallet if there are lots of pages so that the wallet bulges and appears to be full.

Search for suitable buckles for these books. The buckles used here were taken from an old pair of shoes. The buckles need to correspond to the size of the book.

This particular book was made to commemorate a family outing to the Tabernas film set in Spain. This is where the Spaghetti Westerns were made and so the book, using photographs from the visit, needed to have a cowboy feel about it. Cocoon-stripping paper was chosen for the outer cover. This was dyed with coffee and the paper was strengthened with Ormoline. The straps for this wallet-style book were further strengthened with PVA.

The straps undo to reveal the pages in the book. The pages were made from bought suede-effect fabric. This fabric frayed and the edges did not look appealing. To overcome this problem each of the pages was worked separately and then two were placed right sides together and three sides were sewn. The 'bag' was then turned the right way out and the two sides of the open end were turned in. Slipstitch with invisible thread was used to close this side. A pile of pages was assembled and the content worked out prior to stitching. Each page contains a photographed image which has been transferred to Lutradur that was first painted with Golden Digital Ground (see page 58).

The finished pages should be placed in a pile on the cover so that the fold line is off-centre as illustrated above. Invisible thread was used to machine stitch down the fold.

Above and left: This book has a cocoon-stripping cover coloured with coffee and strengthened with Ormoline, and suede-effect fabric pages.

# PROJECT
# Peeled paint on cocoon-stripping paper

The fabric for the reindeer book shown right was made from cocoon-stripping paper. Embossing with an ink pad alone is not recommended for this technique as the powders will not adhere to the ink on the paper fabric.

**You will need:**
- baking parchment
- cocoon strippings
- water and travel spray bottle
- iron
- acrylic gloss medium, or Ormoline or acrylic wax
- tracing paper and pencil
- Funky Foam
- scissors or soldering iron
- Tim Holtz Distress Powder and heat gun
- heat-fixable paint
- background paints of your choice
- acrylic wax
- **Optional:** encaustic wax and encaustic iron or travel iron

1   Make cocoon-stripping paper as described on page 45. Paint the paper with acrylic gloss medium mixed with water or Ormoline or acrylic wax. This will strengthen the paper.

2   Trace your pattern for your stamp onto Funky Foam. Cut the stamp out and add any surface detail. (A soldering iron works well for this technique, or you can use something with a sharp point like a biro to make indentations.) When using a soldering iron, always work in a well-ventilated area and consider using a mask to avoid fume inhalation.

3   Paint heat-fixable paint over the stamp and print your design on the cocoon-stripping paper. I particularly like Stewart Gill paint for this technique as the thick paint holds the embossing powders. (You may find it easier to use an ink pad to stamp the design and then paint over the printed design with heat-fixable paint.)

4   Immediately sprinkle the Distress Powder over the paint. Turn the fabric over and tap off the excess. (I work with empty ice-cream tubs so that the powder goes in that and is not wasted.)

5  Use a heat gun to activate the powder. The powder will set hard and tiny crystals will form. (If your powder blows away it means that you do not have sufficient paint to hold the crystals.)

6  Rub the surface and some of the tiny crystals will rub off.

7  Paint the background with paints of your choice.

8  Paint acrylic wax over the background.

9  Optional: iron encaustic wax over parts of the background.

10  Outline the stamped image in backstitch or the outline stitch of your choice.

Reindeer book with cocoon-stripping paper cover.

# Silk paper over Softsculpt

For this project, the emphasis is on the texture, which is achieved by using heat-mouldable foam for the base fabric. The paper that is placed on top should be thin and lacy in parts so that the textured foam shows through.

**You will need:**
- Softsculpt heat-mouldable foam
- heat gun
- rubber stamp
- 505 repositionable spray glue
- thin, lacy silk paper
- Treasure Gold or bronzing powders
- Funky Foam
- scissors or soldering iron
- **Optional:** encaustic wax and encaustic iron or travel iron
- mulberry or other paper of your choice
- PVA (white craft glue)
- acrylic wax
- Adirondack Alcohol Ink
- beeswax polish
- paper towels

1   Begin by impressing texture into heat-mouldable foam. **Tip:** use a heat gun to heat one area on the foam. Immediately press something with raised detail into the heated foam. A rubber stamp was used here. Leave it in position and gently heat the adjacent area. Speedily remove the stamp and press it into the next heated area. Leave it in position and repeat until the whole of the Softsculpt is impressed.

2   Use 505 repositionable spray glue to bond thin, lacy fabric of your choice to the patterned Softsculpt (red lacy silk paper was used here). Leave some of the areas on the Softsculpt exposed.

3   Use free machine stitching to stitch into the layers.

4   Paint bronzing powder mixed with acrylic wax over the raised surface of the fabric or rub colour such as Treasure Gold into parts of the fabric. Work in a well-ventilated area and wear a mask when working with any powders.

Detail of the front of the Softsculpt book.

**5** Use a stamp of your choice for the central motif. A stamp made from Funky Foam was used here. Draw your design on the Funky Foam and cut it out with scissors or with a soldering iron. If you are using a soldering iron, work on a sheet of glass with the edges protected with masking tape, and work in a well-ventilated area and wear a mask.

**6** Melt encaustic wax on the iron and iron the colour onto the stamp. Place mulberry paper or paper of your choice on top and iron to transfer the image onto the paper. Repeat with the paper placed in different positions (a detail of the central motif is illustrated opposite). Alternatively, ink the stamp and stamp in different positions on paper of your choice.

**7** Use PVA to bond the motif to the front cover or appliqué it in place.

**8** Paint acrylic wax over the whole of the work. Leave it to dry.

**9** Liberally apply Adirondack Alcohol Ink to a piece of wadding and swipe it over the entire piece. This will help to integrate it.

**10** Use paper towels to rub and buff beeswax polish into the piece. If your silk paper was thin enough you will find that the more you rub the more pronounced the impressed pattern will be. Some colour will come off onto the paper towel. Keep applying polish, rubbing and changing the paper towel until the piece glows and the paper towel is clean.

**11** Add a decorated spine at this point, if desired. The book shown here has a glue gun-impressed, painted, stitched, beaded spine with a twisted Softsculpt cord, which acts as a bookmark. The tag on the end is made from impressed glue (see page 68).

Mixed-media book cover using a base of Softsculpt heat-mouldable foam.

# Plaster of Paris

Plaster of Paris is more often associated with sculptors and model makers than mixed-media work, but if used with care and thought you can use it to add texture and dimension to your book covers. Simply mix the white powder with water to create a thick paste, form it into shapes and leave to dry. Obviously a motif made from plaster of Paris cannot be stitched into but you can stitch over it and bead it.

### Making a plaster of Paris motif

The process of making plaster of Paris motifs like the one used on the bottom left of the book shown here is easy.

- Draw your design on Funky Foam.
- Cut out the design.
- Mix the plaster with water and use a glue spatula to apply the plaster to the Funky Foam shape.
- Leave it to dry.
- Paint the shape.
- Couch the shape onto your fabric. Sorbello stitch was used to couch this shape onto the fabric. Beads were added later.

The motif opposite was made for my Donatello book, so called as it was inspired by Donatello's altarpiece at Santa Croce in Florence. This large book (27 x 29cm, 10½ x 11in) with card signatures was made to hold my samples and it explores different techniques both on the cover and inside.

The book has an embroidered spine but the spine has been covered with a stamped silk-paper strip.

A rollergraph tool was used to print the design on copper relief foil and then the copper was embossed and coloured to make the dividing strips on the front cover. The centre button was made from impressed Softsculpt.

The back and front covers were constructed on painted evenweave linen. Stewart Gill Fresco Flakes and gold flakes were trapped in Stewart Gill heat-fixable paint to create this background.

Donatello book. The top-left panel is decorated with
silk paper, the top-right with Funky Foam, the
bottom-left with plaster of Paris and the bottom-
right with canvaswork stitches that have been
painted over.

# Plaster of Paris for texture

Try mixing Plaster of Paris with acrylic paint and applying it to textured furnishing fabric. In use it will crack and flake off. To reduce the possibility of it distressing any further, try painting a coat of acrylic wax over it. In the example below, Plaster of Paris was mixed with water and blue acrylic paint. When it was dry, silver metallic powder was mixed with beeswax furniture polish. This was painted over the blue areas. Black webbing spray was added, then the fabric was crumpled to distress it. Lots of the Plaster of Paris crumbled off. A final coat of acrylic wax helped to prevent it from being distressed to any greater extent. The fabric was stretched in a frame and embroidered. The plaster no longer flakes off.

This book cover was created using plaster of Paris mixed with acrylic paint.

# Inkjet printing

There are many different ways in which to print on fabrics. My preference is for methods which do not appear to be plasticized.

Try not to infringe copyrights when printing onto fabrics, papers and metals. Use your own photographs or try photographing your sketchbook work, printing that and then adding to it.

Cactus. Golden Digital Ground on Lutradur. Holes burnt with a soldering iron.

# Digital Ground medium

Digital Ground medium from Golden can enable you to print on just about every flat surface that you can run through an inkjet printer. There is a matt version suitable for most porous surfaces, a gloss version, which allows more of the underlying material to show through, and a non-porous version suitable for printing on foil or plastic, for example.

The field of flowers opposite was printed onto silk paper. I made the paper using one part acrylic gloss medium to four parts water. If you use cocoon-stripping paper instead then it should first be sealed with acrylic wax or PVA (white craft glue) diluted with water.

- Use a foam pad to apply the solution, which will enhance your prints. Gloss Digital Ground was used here. Ensure that the solution is completely dry before printing.
- If the paper is quite thick you may not need a carrier sheet. If you are in any doubt about the possible fragile nature of your silk paper then it may be a good idea to iron it onto freezer paper prior to printing. If the edges look vulnerable they can be secured by applying masking tape to them.
- Alternatively, if the silk paper has interesting features that are relatively flat, you may want the colour and texture to be more prominent. I was quite disappointed that the solution worked so well that the yellow strands of silk on the paper opposite were completely lost in the printing process.

Golden Digital Ground was also used on the Lutradur fabric illustrated on page 57. The advantage of working with Lutradur is that it can be burnt with a soldering iron, if desired.

Digital Ground painted onto
silk paper, then inkjet
printed and embroidered.

# Lazertran paper

Lazertran decal papers enable you to print a design and then transfer it onto a surface – paper, fabric, ceramic, metal and so on. Images transferred to paper or card can be stitched into. The needle does leave pin marks so you will need to use one with a small eye and a thread that fills the hole. Try:
- Using a stamp to ink on top of the printed image.
- Bonding Angelina fibres or FuseFX over the printed image. Note that if you apply too much heat the paper will buckle.

# Jacquard fabric papers

### Extravorganza
This sheer organza fabric can be printed, stamped or trapped in stonework paints or light moulding paste.

### Cotton
This product is very versatile. In the example shown on the opposite page, the image of the eagle was printed onto the cotton, then coloured with Art

Below left: Bronze bust on gold Lazertran, stamped with fibres added.
Below right: Vase-shaped book with Extravorganza lion. The full piece can be seen on page 34.

Quest Jewel watercolour paint. The backing paper was removed and the fabric was stretched in an embroidery frame and then stitched into. The eagle was cut out and appliquéd to textured mulberry paper, which was then appliquéd to lightweight Vilene (Pellon). The background on the Vilene was made by placing it over a textured rubbing tray and rubbing a Markal Paintstik over it. This was then left to set for 24 hours and then Twinkling H2O paints were painted in the spaces. 505 glue was used to bond the items prior to stitching.

### Silk

In the example below right, the panel with the figures was printed onto silk Jacquard fabric paper, then the backing paper was removed. The vase was drawn and painted black on a piece of brown paper bag. Acrylic wax was painted over the vase and gold flakes and Stewart Gill Fresco Flakes were added. The printed silk panel was placed in position while the acrylic wax was still wet so that the black paint showed through. The vase was bonded to textured pulp paper. The vase and panel were stitched into. Black acrylic paint was painted over the figures. Adirondack Alcohol Ink in Terra Cotta was used to colour the background on the silk. Squeeze the ink onto the fibre end of a Fantastix colouring tool brush point to colour small areas.

Below left: Page from Roman carousel book: eagle printed onto cotton.
Below right: Page from Roman carousel book: panel with figures printed onto silk.

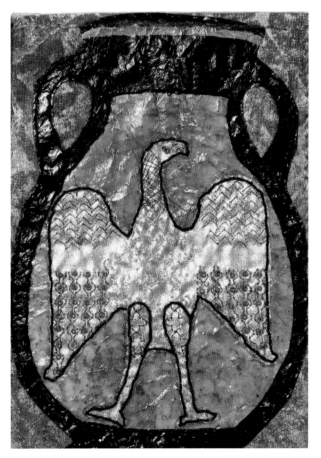

# Silk paper and inkjet prints

Printing your photographs and artwork on silk paper can be exciting. Computer inks used to fade but they are much more stable now. Printing directly onto light-coloured papers produces interesting results because the fibres show through. The silk paper below, depicting the sunset, was printed directly onto beige-coloured de-gummed silk-filament paper.

- Prepare the image you want to print.
- Iron the silk paper onto the shiny side of freezer paper. (You can buy silk paper or make your own. This paper was made by bonding the fibres with a solution of one part acrylic gloss medium to four parts water, making a very strong paper with no loose fibres. Loose fibres are unsuitable for inkjet printing as they could wrap themselves round the rollers.)
- Cut the freezer paper and silk paper to the correct size for your printer. Bind the edges with masking tape, and print the image.
- Remove the freezer paper and the masking tape. Inkjet colours will bleed if moisture is applied, so take care if you are using PVA to bond it to another surface.

Page from 'The Highwayman':
'The moon was a ghostly galleon'.

# Computer inks and lightweight craft Vilene

Lightweight craft Vilene (Pellon) can be stitched into, remains thin enough for multiple pages, can be printed on, stamped, and heat can be applied for embossing. When moisture is applied to inkjet-printed images the colours will run. This characteristic can be exploited in a number of ways.

- Try printing onto lightweight craft Vilene. The image below was reproduced from a photograph.
- Turn the printed image over and use a small paintbrush to paint water sparingly onto selected areas. If you use too much water the inks will muddy in a most unappealing way. Lightweight Vilene is very porous. You only want the ink to run a little so that the photograph resembles an Impressionist painting rather than being a sharp reproduction.
- Consider using silk fibres and a needle-felting Embellisher machine in selected areas as illustrated below.
- Stitch into the fabric. When hand stitching, do not pull the thread too tight or the Vilene will tear. Too many close stitches made by machine stitching may also act as a cutting tool.
- Add colour by rubbing heat-fixable ChromaCoal pastels over some areas and over some stitches.

Remember that the Vilene is porous when you are bonding it to a card page in your book. Use PVA (white craft glue) sparingly or choose glue that does not contain so much moisture.

Page from 'The Highwayman' 'And the highwayman came riding–riding–riding'.

# Inkjet printers and ChromaCoal pastels

ChromaCoal pastels are heat-fixable pastel crayons. A watercolour effect can be achieved by using a combination of computer ink and ChromaCoal pastels. The stages are somewhat reminiscent of 'painting by numbers', but this is a fairly speedy way of illustrating many pages in a book. A paler version of the image will be printed off but this will not be the finished product.

- Print your image off onto lightweight craft Vilene (Pellon) or the background of your choice. Remember not to infringe copyrights. The images for the accordion book (opposite) were taken from holiday photographs and the book commemorates the holidays.
- Use ChromaCoal pastels to highlight certain areas. These are heat-fixable but they should not be heat-fixed at this stage as you want the colours to run and blend. Dab and smudge them and use them sparingly. (If you do not have these pastels try watercolour painting pencils, pastels or chalks. These will need to be fixed later.) Use a rubber to blend the pastel areas and do not worry as they will not look completely blended at this stage.
- For hand stitching, stretch the Vilene in an embroidery sewing frame.
- Stitch into the Vilene. Do not pull the thread too hard or the stitches will tear the Vilene.
- Use the ChromaCoal pastels or chalks over some of the stitches.
- Use PVA (white craft glue) to bond the stitched Vilene to your backing board or card page. It will seep through the Vilene and make a mess so it is advisable to place it on a piece of baking parchment when applying the glue. Do not leave it to dry. Getting the balance right between how much PVA to paint on the Vilene is important as the card page you will bond it to needs to be strong enough to withstand the amount of glue used. It has a tendency to buckle if too much glue is used. I have also found that some brands of PVA are thicker than others. If you use too much PVA it could result in a muddy mess!
- Lift it gently onto your card or fabric. Try not to smudge it and lay it carefully in position.
- Place a piece of baking parchment over it and smooth it out gently with your fingers. I place a heavy object on the baking parchment for about five minutes. Don't leave it on any longer as you do not want the PVA to set and dry with the baking parchment on.
- Carefully remove the weight and the baking parchment. The piece will still be wet. Leave it to dry.
- When it is completely dry the colours will have run and merged. If you wish you could seal the colours by applying a little heat or by painting acrylic wax over the surface. Consider this carefully as you do not want the card page to buckle. Painting acrylic wax over images tends to darken the image.

Pages from the accordion buildings book shown on page 32. Inkjet-printed Vilene pages with ChromaCoal pastels.

# Clear embossing enamel

Stone crosses are part of the landscape on the North Yorkshire moors and I used this as the location for my book 'The Highwayman'. In order to make the stone cross blend into the background, Opals clear embossing enamel by Pipedream (in the 'Franklin' colour) was used. This clear glaze enamelling powder works well when used over inkjet-printed lightweight craft Vilene (Pellon). Any moisture applied to the inkjet-printed image will make the colours run. Ink pads as used by crafters will not work on lightweight Vilene for this technique.

- Print your image onto lightweight Vilene (for the piece in the picture opposite, I used a photograph of a watercolour painting).
- Stitch into the Vilene.
- Print another copy of the photograph onto lightweight Vilene. Paint acrylic wax over the area that will be embossed.
- Immediately sprinkle the Opals clear embossing enamels over the wet acrylic wax. Speed is necessary as the inkjet-printed colours will run and although you want to make use of this you do not want them to run too far.
- Use a heat gun to melt the crystals.
- While the crystals are still hot, sprinkle on more crystals and heat.
- Dust a rubber stamp with talcum powder and place it in the hot crystals. Remove the stamp when the enamels are cold.
- When the enamelled crystals are cold you can cut out shapes of your choice (a stone cross was used here).
- The embossed image can be stitched into. The stone cross was appliquéd to the inkjet-printed image on the Vilene.

Right: 'Back he spurred like a mad man'. Clear embossing enamels over inkjet-printed Vilene. Left: detail of the centre of the cross.

# Glue sticks

Hot-melt or cold glue sticks work for this technique, which relies on reheating the glue. Glue patches can be stitched and beaded. Keep baby wipes handy to clean the needle as you work. Do not touch the hot glue at any point in these procedures.

- Place baking parchment on a hard surface on which you can exert pressure.
- Measure the size of your moulding mat or rubber stamp and draw the rectangle to size on the parchment to act as a guide.
- Heat the hot-melt glue stick and press the trigger to release the glue onto the baking parchment and to cover the marked-out area.
- Use a heat gun to re-heat the glue. Cover the hot glue with baking parchment and iron over it to flatten the glue. You will need to exert pressure. A heavy weight can also be used to iron over and flatten the glue.
- When the glue is cold, remove the baking parchment. If the glue has been flattened, proceed to the next step. If it is still lumpy, repeat and add more glue, if necessary. Any bubbles or marks in the glue will be obliterated at the painting stage.
- Dust a rubber texture mat or stamp with talcum powder.
- Use a heat gun to re-melt the glue.
- Place the rubber texture mat over the hot glue. Take care not to touch the glue. Leave the mat in place until the glue is completely cold.
- Remove the mat. The glue is now ready to paint.

**Tip:** for long-lasting coverage, paint over the glue using Stewart Gill paints and bronzing powders mixed with acrylic wax.

**NB** Work in a well-ventilated place and use a mask if working with bronzing powders.

The glue-patch door opens to reveal an embroidered scene. The glue was painted with gold bronzing powder mixed with acrylic wax.

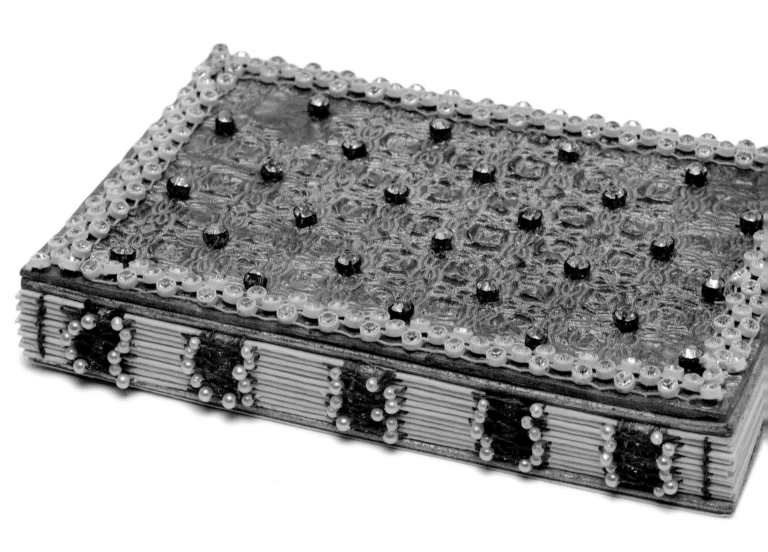

Beaded, textured glue patch on the front of a
book with an embroidered spine. Coloured with
Stewart Gill Byzantia paints and gold bronzing
powder mixed with acrylic wax.

# Using other objects to impress the glue

Wooden carved blocks and metal shapes with designs moulded to them can be used instead of a texture mat to impress glue but they must be protected by a layer of talcum powder.

Experiment with different shapes but take care not to use anything valuable as accidents can occur and the glue may do what it is made for and stick to the object. Do not attempt to remove the object until the glue is completely cold.

Coloured glue patches can be re-heated and re-melted to form larger patches provided that the paint on them is not toxic. I use Stewart Gill heat-fixable paints. Experimenting with painted reconstituted glue can produce some surprising effects. It is possible to produce a marbled-effect pattern that does not need repainting.

The glue patch windows for the Chartres book (below) were made by pressing a metal shape into the glue. The windows are coloured with gold bronzing powder mixed with acrylic wax and are appliquéd to silk paper, which has been coloured and polished to resemble old leather.

The textured glue patch for the Toledo book (opposite), was also coloured with gold bronzing powder but patination fluid was added to age it. Always take care when working with bronzing powders and patination fluid. Work in a well-ventilated area and if possible wear a respirator and mask. If you spill any powder, wipe it up straight away with a wet paper towel. **Note:** Patination fluid only works on wet bronzing powder. Use it sparingly as it only becomes visible when it is dry.

This glue patch was also appliquéd to silk paper but the silk paper was covered with red sheer fabric.

Left: Chartres, featuring windows made of
impressed glue coloured with gold bronzing
powder mixed with wax.
Above: Toledo, also made with textured glue.

# Metal relief foils

Metals or relief foils can be used for book covers or the pages of books. The simplest way in which to emboss metal is to use an old biro, but the most effective way is to use tools that are purpose-made for this technique. It can become very costly, but a basic set of tools is really all that is needed when the focus is colour and stitch. I like to work on aluminium shim or thin relief foil. Aluminium shim colours well with alcohol inks. Relief foils are cheap, easy to colour and stitch into. Relief foil comes in A4 (letterhead-sized) sheets, making it a good size to work with. Although the copper coloured relief foil is only a copper-coloured coating, it can be heated over a gas flame to change the colour if desired. It will get very hot so it is necessary to hold it with tongs and with an oven glove to protect your hands. Alternatively, colour it as explained below.

- Draw your design onto tracing paper. Use masking tape to secure the drawing over a piece of metal relief foil.
- Use the fine tip of an embossing tool to outline the drawing on the tracing paper, then remove the tracing paper and use embossing tools to add detail to the metal. Keep turning the metal over and work on both sides to obtain as much embossed detail as possible. Use a magazine as a working surface.

Page from 'The Highwayman'.
'He'd a bunch of lace at his chin'.

- Consider adding texture to the surrounding area by using the tip of your smallest tool to stipple the metal. These fine little dots will help to make the piece look suitably aged and distressed, especially after it has been painted. Other interesting ways in which you can add texture to the background could be to draw little 'stitches', such as fly-shaped stitches or meandering lines of running stitch.
- When the relief foil has been embossed it should be coloured. Use either black acrylic paint or a dark-coloured glass paint to paint over the whole area. Work quickly and push the paint into the crevices. As soon as you have finished, use a paper towel or piece of kitchen towel to rub the paint off the surface. Do this immediately as you do not want the paint to remain on the surface.
- Fix the glass paint according to the manufacturer's instructions on the packaging, or, working in a well-ventilated area wearing a mask, use a heat tool to set the paint.
- Use Adirondack Alcohol Ink to colour the surface. Either use a piece of wadding to apply the ink to the whole of the surface or use the tip of a Fantastix colouring tool brush. If you are using the brush point tool, squeeze the ink onto it and use it immediately. Wear rubber gloves to protect your hands from the ink.

Page from 'The Highwayman'.
'Where Tim the ostler listened'.

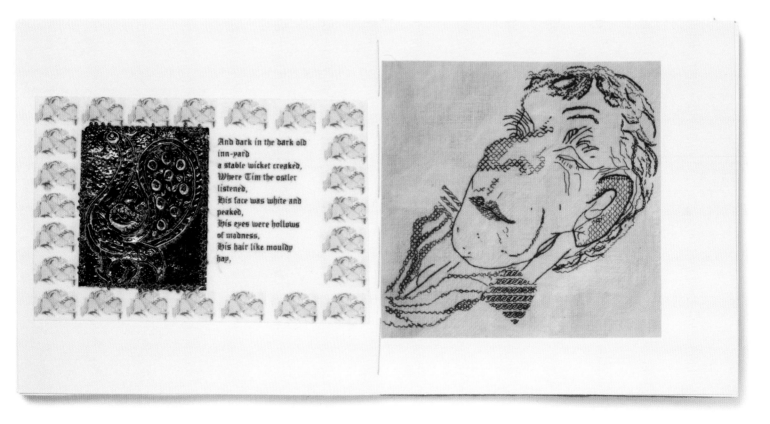

# Inkjet printing on copper relief foil

Products such as Golden Digital Ground or InkAid can be used to prime the surface of shim or foil ready for printing, or a combination of Perfect Paint by Earth Safe and gesso can be used.

### Old World Peasant paint and gesso

With care, A4 (letterhead-sized) sheets of copper relief foil can be inkjet printed if first primed with Perfect Paint by Earth Safe, followed by a coat of white gesso.

- Work only on clean metal.
- The ink will not remain on the Perfect Paint alone. It should be used in conjunction with gesso. Allow each layer to dry thoroughly before applying the next. Begin with a thin layer of Perfect Paint.
- Paint a thin layer of white gesso. Do not make a thick layer of gesso or it will pull and tear off when you emboss the metal. I have experimented with cheap gesso and the more expensive varieties. It works with both but needless to say the more expensive variety is always the best.
- Bind all of the edges of the copper relief foil with masking tape so that they do not damage the print head. Copper relief foil is A4 in size and I found that by following these guidelines I was able to obtain large prints. Do not use your inkjet printer for this technique if you are worried about possible accidents. It may be worth investing in a cheap printer which is reserved for experimental work.
- You may wonder if it is worth all of this effort. The reason that I like it is that the use of the Perfect Paint enables you to sand the resulting image. The printed image on the metal should be embossed prior to sanding so that the raised areas only are sanded back.

The metal image opposite was partially embossed and stitched. Perfect Paint was used on the background paper. See paint and scrub, page 114, for further details.

Bess – Earth Safe Perfect Paint and gesso on inkjet-printed metal. Perfect Paint was used on the background (see paint and scrub, page 114).

# Printing on aluminium and copper foil

A more straightforward way of inkjet printing on metals is to use Golden Digital Ground or InkAid.

- Use a foam pad or roller to apply the Digital Ground or InkAid for non-porous surfaces. Use of a paintbrush could result in unsightly streaking.
- When it is completely dry the metal should be attached to a carrier sheet. Use masking tape to attach the sheet to computer paper. The use of masking tape is necessary to eliminate the possible risk of sharp edges damaging the print head.

### Mylar Shimmer Sheetz
- The two images below were printed onto Mylar Shimmer Sheetz which were first primed with Digital Ground for non-porous surfaces.
- The Mylar was attached to a computer-paper carrier sheet using masking tape, as described above.
- The Mylar was inkjet printed.
- The image on the right was placed on a spongy mouse mat and heated with a heat gun. A large wooden stamp was pressed into the Mylar to emboss it.

Below left: Print on gold Mylar Shimmer Sheetz.
Below right: Green Mylar Shimmer Sheetz printed and embossed.

# Coloured gesso on copper relief foil

Interesting effects can be achieved by combining Old World Peasant paint with coloured paints and gesso.

- Paint copper relief foil with a thin layer of Old World Peasant paint, leaving a few hairline streaks of the copper to remain visible.
- When the paint is dry, apply paint on top. I applied streaks of red, yellow and blue paint.
- Apply a thin layer of white gesso over the coloured paints, when they are almost dry but still a little tacky. In this case, the gesso partially obliterated the colour but streaks of coloured paint were still visible. When all of the paint is completely dry, an image can be printed onto the metal using an inkjet printer. The edges of the A4 sheet of copper relief foil should be bound with masking tape so that they do not damage the print head.
- I left the copper for one day and then sanded it lightly to distress it and reveal the layers.

Herculaneum. Fresco with Roman senator in copper relief foil.

# Texture with Golden Fiber Paste

Making your own pulp papers and adding texture as you work is by far the cheapest way in which to create unique surfaces. If you do not want to go down this route, there are many ready-made products that you can use as alternatives that give exciting effects. Fiber Paste by Golden is a thick paste that can be applied to papers and fabrics using a palette knife or plastic glue spreader. If you skim the surface with a wet knife you can make it smoother, but I prefer to use it to create peaks and troughs. When it is dry it has a tough finish that can be painted and which feels like card. It can be stitched into.

There are a few ways in which you can use this product to create texture. The technique used to make the book cover illustrated opposite relies on using a rubber texture mat. I worked on Lokta pulp paper because it is cheap and because it is an ideal thickness for book covers, but you could work on papers or fabrics of your choice.

- Begin by spreading a generous layer of Fiber Paste over your paper. I used a plastic glue spreader for this.
- Push something textured into the wet paste. This is a messy process and you should consider carefully what you would like to use; it needs to be something that you can wash after use. I used an A5-sized (8 x 5in) rubber texture mat and repeated the process until the A4-sized sheet of Lokta paper was textured. Wash your texturing item immediately as you do not want the paste to dry in the crevices.
- When the paste is dry it can be coloured. You can use paints of your choice for this. As I was working on the theme of water and water-skiing I used the paint-and-scrub technique described on pages 114–117 to capture the feel of a Mediterranean sea. Earth Safe Perfect Paint was used as a primer and sealer and then it was painted using a combination of Stewart Gill, Seraphym, Willow Blue and Fra Angelico paints. When all the paint was thoroughly dry, it was sanded to reveal the white foam created by the splash.
- The coloured paper can be stitched into. I prefer to do this when it is flat and stretched, but since it is textured anyway it would not matter too much if it got creased and crumpled. Papers can be bonded to cotton quilter's wadding (batting) or lightweight Vilene (Pellon) prior to stitching. If you stitch into Lokta paper without using a backing then you may need to secure the ends of threads with masking tape.

Splash. Lokta pulp paper with Golden Fiber Paste and Evolon fabric marbled with the tilt-and-run method (see page 100).

# Fiber Paste on mulberry paper

Added texture can be achieved by raising the surface by bonding one piece of textured paper to another, and by using Fiber Paste on top of that.

a

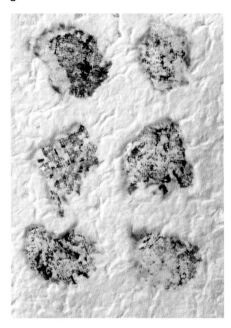

**You will need:**
- mulberry or textured paper
- 505 spray glue
- two or more sticks of encaustic wax – one should be gold
- encaustic iron or travel iron
- Brusho paint or any thin paint
- Golden Fiber Paste
- glue spatula
- cotton quilter's wadding (batting)
- embroidery frame
- embroidery thread (variegated fine silk was used here)
- baking parchment
- ironing board
- grey board
- book block

1 Tear rough circles or discs out of mulberry paper. The circles illustrated opposite were torn from mulberry paper which had been coloured by cleaning encaustic wax off an encaustic iron between processes (a).

2 Glue the discs to another piece of textured mulberry paper. Swipe encaustic wax down an encaustic iron and iron it over the paper.

b

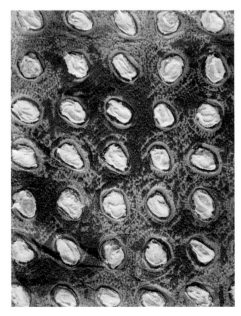

3 Paint the background with Brusho or any thin paint, then use a spatula to smear Fiber Paste over the discs (b). When the paste is dry, bond the paper to cotton quilter's wadding with 505 spray glue.

4 Stretch the paper in a frame and stitch into the paper. (Fly stitch was embroidered round the discs using variegated fine silk.) The paper can be machine-stitched if desired, in which case you will not need a frame.

5 Protect the ironing board with baking parchment and place the paper on the parchment. Swipe encaustic wax down the iron and iron over the raised surfaces of the paper. Repeat with colours of your choice.

6 Iron gold encaustic wax over the raised surfaces on the paper.

7 Cut the paper to size and bond it to grey board. Make a book block and bond the covers to the endpapers.

Fiber Paste discs on mulberry paper, decorated with
embroidery and encaustic wax.

# Texture effects

Embroidered pages for books can become unwieldy. For many of the pages in my embroidered story books I have used altered lightweight Vilene (Pellon), which has been embroidered and bonded to card folios. Occasionally I have found it necessary to work on a heavier Vilene in order to use mixed-media techniques that rely on the use of a heat gun. The page opposite is an illustration from my book 'The Highwayman', and it was worked on pelmet Vilene. This heavy version was necessary because I intended to use peeled-paint embossing powders for the shutters and I did not want the page to buckle under the intense heat needed for this.

## Pastel crayons, Tyvek and Fresco Flakes

The following technique was used to create the crumbling stucco or rendered wall that I wanted for the exterior of the house shown opposite. You can use the same technique to create the stonework of any building.

- I used ChromaCoal pastels for the background. You could also try pastels or watercolour pencils as an alternative to heat-fixable ChromaCoal pastels. Rub the pastels over the back of the Vilene.
- Use a paintbrush and water to paint over the pastels. The water will run into the colour and make it bleed. As the colours bleed and blend they will seep through the Vilene, colouring the front. By applying the pastels to the back you will achieve a mottled, muted appearance.
- Distress a sheet of Tyvek by ironing it between two sheets of baking parchment.
- Tear it to distress it further and stitch it in place on the walls.
- Use Ormoline or acrylic wax to paint over the walls. Trap Stewart Gill Fresco Flakes in the wet fabric medium to represent the crumbling surface of the walls.
- Place black FuseFX over the walls. Cover it with baking parchment and iron it to bond it in position.

'He tapped with his whip on the shutters.'
Page from 'The Highwayman'.

# Pop-up stone castle

The pop-up page shown below was made across two pages of lightweight Vilene. The outer wall of the castle is made to look like stucco, and the interior like plaster. To create the stucco walls, the paint-and-scrub technique described on page 114 was used. Black fusible webbing was then ironed on after the walls had been sanded. The walls for the interior were created by printing ancient script onto tea-bag paper. The tea-bag paper was first ironed onto freezer paper, which was then used as a carrier sheet for the inkjet printing process. Clear encaustic wax was ironed over the printed tea-bag paper and it was then embroidered. It was ironed again to remove any pinprick holes (see page 106). Windows were cut on the outer page so that a glimpse of the girl within could be seen. About 2cm (1in) of the reverse left and right sides of the outer page were covered with PVA (white craft glue) and they were bonded in position over the page below, so that when the page is opened it has a 3-D effect.

Room with a View.

# DecoArt Sandstones

I quite like using this product in conjunction with inkjet-printed images, as the ink can be used to colour the stonework. Try working on computer-printable cotton or lightweight Vilene (Pellon).

- Print your design onto the fabric.
- Use a plastic glue spreader to apply the paste to your chosen area. This wet mixture will make the ink bleed and this in turn will seep into the sandstone mixture, colouring it. To aid this process, try painting water over the back of your fabric to make the colours run further and give it an aged appearance.
- Things can be trapped in the mixture while it is still wet. Try trapping sheer fabrics or Extravorganza that has been ink jet printed.
- Marks and indentations can be made by using a pointed stick while the paste is still wet.

Stonework pages from the Roman carousel book. Water was painted on the back of the building, and the background of the stone lion was painted black to obliterate any blemishes.

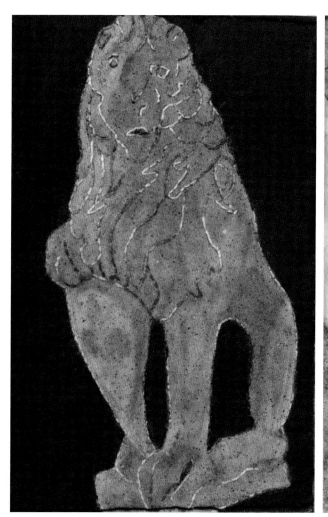

# Translucent Liquid Sculpey with DecoArt Sandstones

Translucent Liquid Sculpey (TLS) is liquid polymer clay that comes in a bottle. The book cover opposite was made by using DecoArt Sandstones on top of Translucent Liquid Sculpey paper.

In the example opposite, the TLS paper was made by baking three layers of Sculpey on a sheet of glass.

- Paint the Sculpey onto a sheet of glass using a dedicated paintbrush. (When you have finished, wrap the paintbrush in a polythene bag so that it is reusable on another occasion.)
- Bake the Sculpey following the manufacturer's instructions.
- Use a Gelly Roll pen to draw on the baked Sculpey or print your design onto this TLS paper using a bought or homemade stamp and a StazOn ink pad.
- Bake the Sculpey for a second time to set the images.
- Paint another layer of Sculpey over the first layer. Bake again to trap the images between these two layers of Sculpey.
- Decide whether to paint a third layer of Sculpey and bake it or whether to proceed with the next stage. A lot will depend on how thick your first two layers are: I used three thin layers here.
- Use a scalpel to remove the TLS paper from the glass. Lift the edges and it will peel straight off.
- Use Adirondack Alcohol Inks to colour areas, if desired. I coloured the windows with Alcohol Inks. The inks do not need to be heat-set.
- Use a glue spatula to spread the DecoArt textural acrylic stonework paste over selected areas of the TLS and leave it to dry.
- The stonework can be left as it is or coloured using any paints. I used terracotta Alcohol Ink to shade the stonework.
- When the paint is dry it can be stitched into.
- The areas around the arched windows were roughly stitched in fly stitch and then white gesso was painted over the sandstone and stitches. A wet baby wipe was used to blend the gesso so that it did not obliterate everything.

## 3-D effects

Products can be bought which are used by crafters to achieve three-dimensional effects, such as double-sided foam mounting tape, which can be given an extra layer of PVA to ensure that it stays in place. Sometimes it is good to improvise with what you already have. The brickwork arch shown opposite, made on cotton fabric, was raised by using double-sided sticky tape and PVA on draught excluder.

Memories of Florence. Book cover using DecoArt Sandstones on Translucent Liquid Sculpey with inkjet-printable cotton panel.

# Molding Paste on textured Lokta pulp paper

This technique involves pressing objects, in this case lace, into wet texture paste. Work on Lokta pulp paper.

- Spread Golden Light Molding paste in the area where you want the lace.
- Use your fingers to press strips of lace into the wet paste. Immediately, but carefully, remove the lace.
- Wet the rest of the Lokta paper with water.
- Place it on a wooden board.
- Hammer the areas not covered by the paste. Use the 'dots' tip of a Tim Holtz texture hammer or a kitchen tool with texture such as a spaghetti server.
- Allow the paper to dry.
- Paint Perfect Paint by Earth Safe over the whole of the paper.
- Allow the paint to dry and then apply paints of your choice.
- When the paints are dry, sand the paper to distress it.
- Iron tea-bag paper onto freezer paper.
- Print your design on the tea-bag paper. You may need to protect the edges with masking tape, depending on your printer.
- Peel the tea-bag paper off the freezer paper. If the paper is reluctant to come off then you should leave it in place. The image opposite had the freezer paper removed.
- Use 505 to bond the tea-bag paper to the textured Lokta paper. Press the paper in position using your fingers. If you have removed the freezer paper the textured surface on the Lokta paper should show through.
- Use acrylic wax to seal the tea-bag paper. This will darken the image and it will also make the colours run and blend and take up some of the background colour. If you do not want the colour to run then proceed to the next stage.
- Stitch into the image and the surrounding paper.
- Iron clear encaustic wax over the whole of the paper to integrate the piece.
- Bond the paper to grey board.
- Sew a book block to the appropriate size.
- Bond the Lokta paper to the book block.

Fleeing from Pompeii. Stone statue on Lokta pulp paper.

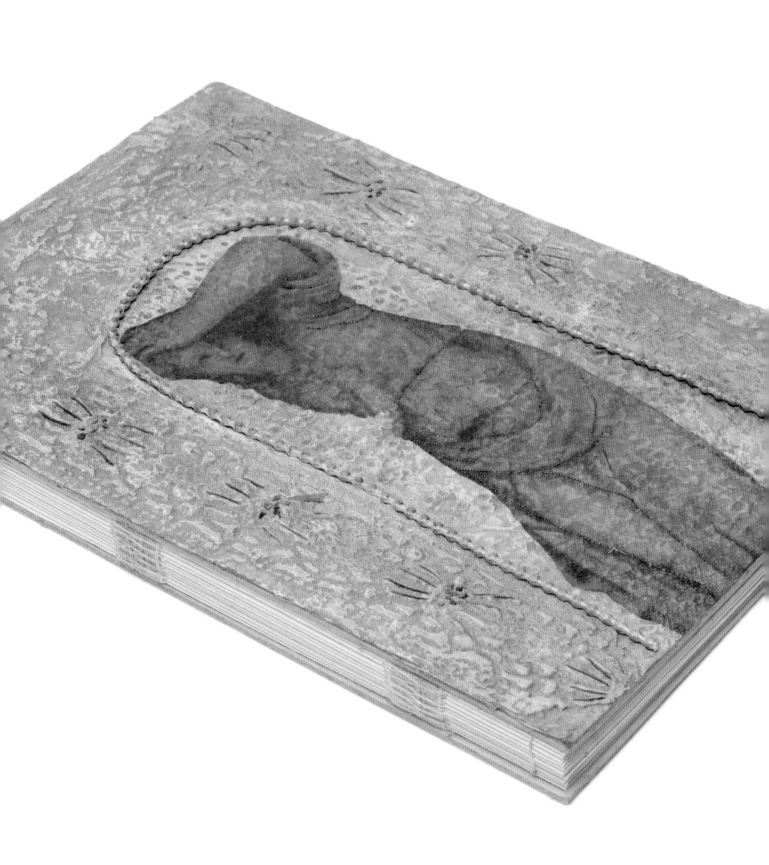

# Light Molding Paste and Distress Crackle Paint

A combination of Golden Light Molding Paste and Distress Crackle Paint by Tim Holtz was used to create the book cover shown on the opposite page. I experimented with lightweight Craft Vilene (Pellon), silk paper, calico and computer-printable cotton fabric by Jacquard. The molding paste is quite thick and it has a tendency to make the fabric buckle as it dries if you use too much. The silk paper I was using buckled on my first attempt as it was not porous. I found that it works well on lightweight Craft Vilene, computer-printable cotton papers and calico backed with a carrier paper. The backing on the carrier paper helps to stabilize the fabric and reduces buckling. The backing papers should be removed when the Molding Paste is dry. This product remains easy to stitch into.

- Iron calico or light cotton fabric onto freezer paper or use Jacquard computer-printable cotton fabric. I used the latter for the book shown opposite.
- Draw or print your design onto your chosen fabric. Leave the backing paper in place. Leave a border round your image to enable you to embroider it at a later stage. The cotton illustrated here was later stretched in an embroidery frame to facilitate the stitching.
- Use a plastic glue spatula to spread the Light Molding Paste over the image. I tried to keep the paste flat as I wanted texture but not peaks.
- When it is dry, use the thick brush applicator, which is in the Distress Crackle Paint bottle, to apply a light coat of paint to your chosen area. A light coating will give you small hairline cracks as can be seen at the top of the doorway. Heavier application will result in deeper cracks, which are prone to splitting, as can be seen down the left-hand side of the doorway. I also used a small paintbrush to control where the paint went as it is a thick medium to work with. The crackle paint I used was already green in colour.
- Leave it to dry. Cracks will appear as it dries.
- Rub a pad of Tim Holtz Distress Ink over the image. This will go into the cracks to age the effect and it will also knock back the colour.
- Paint the rest of your image. I used acrylic paints.
- Remove the backing paper.
- The image can be stitched and beaded, if desired.

Doorway in Light Molding Paste with Distress Crackle Paint.

# Cotton fabric, Molding Paste, Distress Crackle Paint and Distress Ink

Inspired by a vase which is in the Alhambra, this book has a crazed glaze effect. The spine is sewn on the left hand side and is only 4cm (1½in) long. As the length of the book is 28cm (11in) it required an additional method to hold it together when it was closed. This was achieved by threading imitation leather cords with large beads attached through the handle of the vase. By tying these cords loosely it makes a decorative feature but it also holds the book in line. When they are untied the book opens out flat.

- Iron cotton fabric onto freezer paper.
- Draw the image on the fabric.
- Spread Light Molding Paste over the image. I spent a considerable amount of time smoothing it out with the aid of a plastic glue spreader.
- When it is dry, apply Tim Holtz Distress Crackle Paint. I used the blue Broken China colour. Once dry, rub a pad of Distress Ink over the image.
- I found that the light blue colour needed to be knocked back further in order to achieve the aged appearance that I wanted. I used Adirondack Alcohol Ink in Blue Denim to do this.
- Add further details. I drew and painted the two animals.
- Remove the backing paper.
- Bond the cotton fabric to lightweight Vilene (Pellon) with 505 spray glue and stretch it in an embroidery frame to stitch and bead it.
- The shapes on the handle and the centre bottom were made from tea-bag paper which was coloured and appliquéd to the base fabric.

Detail of the front of the book.

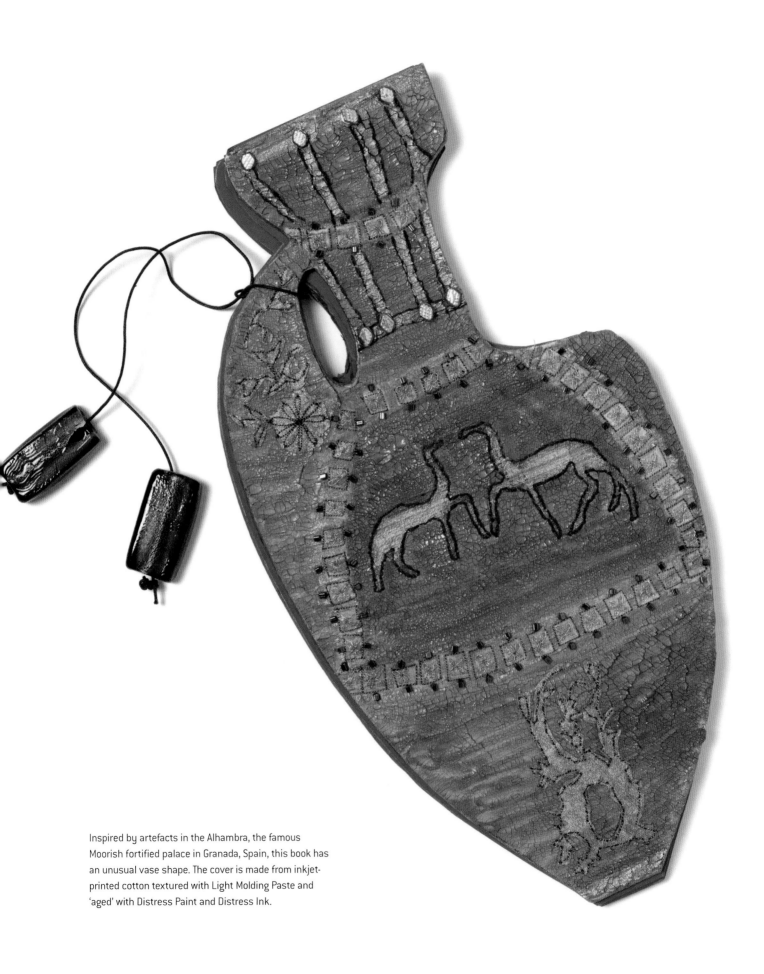

Inspired by artefacts in the Alhambra, the famous Moorish fortified palace in Granada, Spain, this book has an unusual vase shape. The cover is made from inkjet-printed cotton textured with Light Molding Paste and 'aged' with Distress Paint and Distress Ink.

## Raku

Attempting to reproduce a fired-earth raku-type fabric without using a kiln resulted in the books illustrated below.

Fired Earth, the book on top, was worked on Japanese rice paper but this paper does not necessarily have to be used for this technique. The fabric for this book was heavily stitched into and the mixed-media techniques were worked on top of the stitches.

- Colour Japanese rice paper. I used blue silk dye.
- Colour Bondaweb (Wonder Under) and use it to bond a sheer fabric to the rice paper.
- Bond the rice paper to pelmet Vilene (Pellon).
- Stitch as desired. This piece was stitched into using free machine stitching and hand stitching.
- Add further paint as desired. I applied Tim Holtz Distress Crackle Paint in the Old Paper colour over selected areas of the paper and left it to dry.
- I rubbed a Distress Ink pad over the Crackle Paint.
- Then I rubbed on ChromaCoal pastels and ordinary pastels.
- Seal the surface – I used Ormoline fabric medium.
- Finally, I dabbed on Alcohol Ink in Blue Denim in some areas.

A similar technique was used for the Caverns book. This was worked on silk paper and the instructions above were followed.

Large book: Caverns.
Small book: Fired Earth.

Paysage marin,
le seul où je sois libre,
Qui parle mieux qu'un homme,
avec plus de grandeur
Donne-moi, pour un soir,
cette raison de vivre.

Odilon- Jean Perier

## Distress Inks

When water is sprayed onto these inks they run and create an aged effect, and as a result they can make great backgrounds. The background for the page illustrated above was made on lightweight craft Vilene (Pellon).

- I began by painting the verse onto the Vilene.
- The Vilene was scrunched up into a ball, opened out and Distress Ink was rubbed over it.
- The blue silk-paper panel with the copper relief foil letter was sewn in position.
- An acorn stamp was inked up on the blue Distress Ink pad and the acorn border was stamped onto the Vilene.
- Normally water would be sprayed onto the Vilene to activate the distress properties of the ink and then it would be ironed, but in this instance PVA (white craft glue) was used to bond the piece to the card page. The PVA seeped through the lightweight material and activated the distress properties of the ink.

Page from the Donatello book. Tim Holtz Distress Ink on lightweight Vilene. Lutradur bookmark.

# Marbling

Marbling is an ancient craft that started in the twelfth century and soared in popularity in the nineteenth century. Different methods of marbling on fabrics are still being explored by textile artists today. The techniques outlined in this book rely on suspending paints or dyes on beds of shaving foam, Ormoline or PVA.

Evolon is a new microfilament fabric that you can paint, dye and print onto, making it a good choice for your marbling experiments. It is porous and quickly soaks up the colours. It is an interesting fabric to work with as it does not fray, can be cut with a soldering iron and it can also withstand heat from a heat gun or iron. This means that it can also be used for other mixed-media techniques as explored on the following pages. Book covers using Evolon will be tactile as this fabric resembles suede.

## Shaving-foam prints

This is quite messy so you will need to prepare your work surface before you begin. You will need a wide container to hold the shaving foam, Evolon fabric and paints or dyes in your chosen colours.

### Method
- Squirt the shaving foam into the container. It needs to be a thin layer. Use the spatula to spread the foam as evenly as possible in the container.

- Drop small patches of colour onto the foam (silk dye is used here).

- Use a pointed stick to swirl the colours into a pattern. How the colours merge will depend upon the type of paint or dye used.

- Place the Evolon fabric on top. Lay it lightly on the surface and pat it gently so that the fabric touches the whole of the surface (the colour should begin to show through before you remove it).

- Carefully remove the fabric. Place it on a flat surface and use a spatula to scrape the excess shaving foam off gently. The foam will come off but the coloured pattern will remain. Leave to dry.

Experimenting with various types of paints or dyes will produce different effects as some paints and dyes blend as opposed to marbling. You can also try using this technique with other fabrics and papers.

Below: Patches of silk dye dropped onto shaving foam. Bottom: A sheet of Evolon fabric laid over the shaving foam.

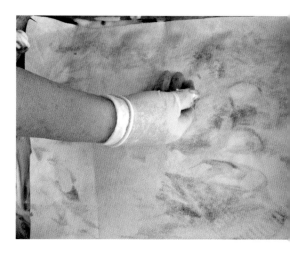

Marbled Evolon bonded to Grungeboard, with
free-machine stitching through the Evolon
and Grungeboard and a hand-stitched
border.

# Marbled Evolon and fusible film

Heat-fixable paints and dyes can be fixed by ironing the marbled Evolon.
Try using some of these techniques to enhance your artwork further:

- Cut out shapes from the marbled Evolon. Use scissors or a soldering
  iron to cut the shapes out. Work in a well-ventilated area when using
  soldering irons and wear a mask, if necessary. The resulting shapes can
  be appliquéd to another fabric.
- Place the marbled Evolon over Kunin felt. Use a soldering iron to cut
  the shapes out. The Evolon will bond to the Kunin felt. Do not burn
  through to the glass or tile that you are working on as you do not want
  to burn through the Kunin felt. Remove the excess Evolon. The
  Evolon shapes will be bonded to the felt. Try burning marks or stitching
  into the fabric.
- Place Stewart Gill Glitterati fusible film or Angelina fusible film over
  the marbled Evolon shapes on the Kunin felt. Burn round the outline
  of the Evolon shapes. Remove the fusible film from the top of the
  marbled shapes. Cover with another sheet of baking parchment and use
  a hot iron to bond the fusible film to the Kunin felt. Watch carefully
  when fusing the film as prolonged intense heat will alter the colour.
- Place the marbled Evolon on a sheet of glass. Cover with fusible film.
  Draw onto the film using a soldering iron to draw tiny shapes and
  squiggles. Place a metal shape over the film. Use the soldering iron in a
  vertical position to cut out the metal shapes. Stitch into these shapes
  and appliqué them to another fabric.

Sometimes the back of the marbled fabric lends itself to these techniques so
it is worth considering both sides before trying mixed-media techniques.

Marbling experiments book. Shaving-foam and silk-dyed marbled Evolon shapes bonded to Kunin felt and Glitterati fusible film.

# Tilt-and-run marbling

I quite like this technique because you are in control of the resulting pattern. You need to use a substance that will run slowly and be easy to use on the fabric. Ormoline fabric medium is not a cheap option but it does work well and can easily be stitched into when the fabric is dry. PVA (white craft glue) is less expensive but it will result in a stiffer, more unappealing fabric. The choice of paints will also affect the end result. You need to use a paint which will run slowly and mix with the other colours without puddling. (**Tip:** Use a pointed stick to help it to run, if necessary.)

You will get more than one print and so you need to have lots of papers or fabrics at hand. Sometimes the last ones are the best!

### Ormoline and Earth Safe paints

Earth Safe Colorant paints come with a pipette inside the bottle so that drops of paint can be applied and mixed with varying solutions. They are very concentrated and work well used in conjunction with Ormoline fabric medium or PVA. Wear gloves to prevent staining your hands and, when the fabric is dry, seal it with acrylic wax, if necessary, as these paints are not colourfast. You could use any dyes or paints for this method but if you experiment you will find that acrylic paints tend to blend as opposed to running and marbling.

Tea-bag paper marbled with Ormoline and Earth Safe Colorant paints. The colour was sealed with acrylic wax and the fish was made from silk paper.

For tilt-and-run marbling, you will need to assemble a large tray, some Ormoline fabric medium or PVA (white craft glue), fabric or paper of your choice, two or more colours of Earth Safe Colorant paint, and a piece of baking parchment. Use the following method:

- Pour a thin layer of Ormoline or PVA into a tray.
- Squeeze the pipette that comes inside the bottle of Colorant paint and place droplets on the Ormoline or PVA (green and blue were used in the example illustrated below.)
- Tilt the tray and watch the droplets of paint run and merge. Keep turning the tray to control the paint run. If you need to add more Ormoline or PVA it is OK to do this. Use a pointed stick to move the paint on a little, if necessary.
- Place the fabric or paper of your choice over the pattern in the tray. Gently pat it, if necessary. The pattern should appear on the back before you remove it.
- Remove the paper and place it face up on the baking parchment.
- Use a spatula dedicated to this job to scrape the Ormoline or PVA and paint off the fabric. The pattern will remain on the fabric.
- Return the excess paint to the tray and transfer paint to different fabrics of your choice.
- Leave the papers or fabrics to dry on baking parchment.

Earth Safe paints marbled on Ormoline. The spine is distressed with the paint-and-scrub method (see page 114).

# Marbling twice with the tilt-and-run method

If you use all of the paint in the marbling tray, not all of your experiments will be to your liking. If you do not like any of the experiments you can always paint over the fabric with gesso and start again. Or you could try marbling the fabric again in a different paint run.

The Evolon fabric opposite was first dyed in the acrylic paint shown below. The acrylic paint is floating on a bed of PVA. The resulting fabric was most unappealing. It was stiff and the pattern was not to my liking. Rather than abandon it, I decided to marble it for a second time. I dropped green and blue Earth Safe Perfect Paint into a tray containing Ormoline fabric medium. The tray was tilted until the colours marbled. The Evolon fabric was coloured for the second time by placing it in the paint tray and then removing the excess paint by scraping it off with a spatula as described on page 101.

### Sheer fabrics
Changes can also be made by placing a sheer fabric over the marbled Evolon and stitching randomly into it. If you are going to use a soldering iron to remove sheer fabric, then metallic thread or thread that will not burn should be used. To remove excess sheer fabric, slide a needle into it and use a soldering iron to burn against the needle.

The acrylic paint floating on a bed of PVA (white craft glue).

Evolon fabric marbled twice, with sheer
fabric applied in certain areas and machine
and hand stitching added.

# Working with waxes

Wax can be used as a bonding agent for embossing powders, or as a barrier before marbling takes place.

## Waxing, marbling and embossing

Try using the following technique to bond embossing enamels with encaustic wax:

- Marble some Evolon fabric using the technique described on page 100.
- When it is dry, use an encaustic iron or a travel iron to iron clear encaustic wax over the fabric. Work on an ironing board protected with baking parchment.
- When the fabric is saturated with the wax, use a heat gun to re-melt the wax.
- Sprinkle Opals Clear Embossing Enamels over the hot wax.
- Shake off the excess powdered crystals and return them to the jar.
- Use a heat gun to melt the crystals.

Clear embossing powders can be used but I particularly like the effect that the Opals embossing enamel gives. All this will remain easy to stitch into.

## Using wax as a resist

Using clear encaustic wax as a barrier can produce some interesting effects. Try working on tea-bag paper or bookbinders' tissue.
- Iron clear encaustic wax over your paper.
- Marble the paper using the shaving-foam method described on page 96. The pattern will only transfer to certain areas because the wax will act as a resist.
- Use a heat gun to heat the paper and melt the wax.
- Sprinkle Opals Franklin Clear Embossing Powder over the hot wax and shake off the excess crystals.
- Heat using a heat gun.

Faces. Waxed, marbled and embossed tea-bag paper.

# Printing and waxing on tea-bag paper

Tea-bag paper works well with this technique because it has subtle texture. However, until it is waxed it is fragile and to overcome this problem freezer paper can be used as a carrier paper. I do not recommend using computer paper with double-sided tape as a carrier paper because there is a possibility that the tea-bag paper could tear and foul up the mechanism in the printer and cause a paper jam. Getting the level of heat right is important as you will not be able to remove the freezer paper if the teabag paper is firmly bonded. If it is difficult to remove the freezer paper then proceed with it in place as the tea-bag paper will still retain its texture.

**Method:**
- Cut freezer paper to A4 (letterhead) size.
- Iron a large sheet of tea-bag paper onto the freezer paper.
- Use masking tape to bind the edges of the freezer paper, to ensure that the tea-bag paper does not get caught in the printer mechanism.
- Use an inkjet printer to print your image.
- Remove the masking tape.
- Remove the freezer paper if you are able.
- Use a travel iron or encaustic iron to iron clear encaustic wax over the printed image.
- Use 505 glue to bond the tea-bag paper to cotton quilter's wadding.
- Stitch into the paper using a needle with a small eye so that large holes do not appear.
- Place baking parchment over the paper and iron it with a clean iron to re-melt the wax and cover any needle holes.

Inkjet-printed images were used for the covers for the two books opposite. They formed part of a study of a Spanish field. Try printing photographs or photographs of your sketchbook work as illustrated. This printing and waxing method was also used to make the fabric for the walls behind the stonework castle on page 84.

Different responses to a Spanish field. Inkjet-printed images of sketchbook work were used as the basis for these book-cover designs. A coating of clear encaustic wax seals the image and adds a soft sheen.

# Encaustic wax over raised surfaces

Materials can be found in the most unexpected places: a kitchen paper towel was used as fabric for this book cover.

- Melt encaustic wax on an encaustic iron or a travel iron without steam vents.
- Iron the melted wax over the textured paper towel.
- Paint the background with paints of your choice. Twinkling H20 paints, Brusho and other thin paints are suitable. Acrylic paint is too thick and will obliterate any pattern.
- Paint acrylic wax over the paper.
- Bond the paper to cotton wadding or lightweight Vilene (Pellon) and stitch into it and bead it.

Encaustic wax ironed over a kitchen paper towel; background painted with Twinkling H20 paints, placed over quilter's wadding and stitched. The bookmark has a paper clay button on the end of the ribbon.

# Wax over stitches and fabric

After all the work involved in hand stitching on evenweave canvas, it takes some courage to wax and paint over the stitches as it can be unpredictable and it changes the work quite dramatically. Sealing it with acrylic wax and ironing encaustic wax over it does, however, change the hue and can knock back the colour so you need to be prepared for this to happen.

Experiments made by sealing crewelwork stitches were unsuccessful and I came to the conclusion that this technique works best over fabric which does not have thick yarns which raise the surface too high.

- Begin by sealing the surface. You could use acrylic wax or Jo Sonja's All-Purpose Sealer, as I used here. The latter leaves a very tough surface.
- When it is dry, melt clear encaustic wax on an encaustic iron or travel iron and iron it onto the fabric.
- If you are happy with the results do not proceed any further. Alternatively, you could rub and buff beeswax polish into it or stitch into it again as illustrated on the book below left. Note that the needle has pushed some of the clear wax to the surface on the red flowers. I wanted this effect so I left it as it is. If you do not want the wax pinpricks to show, iron the fabric and the wax will melt and sink into the holes.
- If you want to add other areas of colour using encaustic wax, melt the wax on the iron and use a dedicated paintbrush to paint the melted wax on the desired areas. Gold encaustic wax was painted over the 'lollipop trees' on the book cover shown right.

The left-hand book has visible clear wax needle holes, while the right-hand book has lollipop-style trees painted with wax.

# Wax and paint over stitch

Painting and waxing over stitches can produce some unusual and unpredictable results. There are so many ways in which you can alter a piece. If you experiment and do not like what you see don't abandon it. There are ways in which to rectify things, even if you have to resort to painting it with gesso and starting again.

- Stitch into your paper or fabric. You can stitch by hand or machine but you are looking for a raised surface so the stitches need to be quite dense. I find that this technique works better with thin threads rather than thick yarns. See the picture below.
- Use encaustic wax to iron over the surface. Most of the wax will be deposited on the stitches but some will inevitably go into some spaces.
- Use paint of your choice to paint the background. (Stewart Gill paints were used here.)
- When it is dry, paint acrylic wax over the fabric.
- Iron encaustic wax over the fabric. Dark blue was used here.
- Rub beeswax polish into the fabric and buff.
- Place the fabric face up on the baking parchment. Iron encaustic wax on again (gold was used here). When you have used beeswax polish on the fabric you will find that the wax runs easily over the surface. Watch carefully to control the amount used.
- Rub a little beeswax polish over the surface and buff again to seal the waxes and create a smooth sheen.

**Tip:** use any of the wax that has been deposited on the baking parchment by placing another piece of paper over it and ironing. The wax will be transferred. This technique works well to give a hint and gleam of wax to cocoon-stripping papers. For a rustic, aged appearance paint the cocoon-stripping pages with diluted coffee and iron them dry over the gold, waxed baking parchment.

Above: Detail of the cross-stitch embroidery on the piece opposite.

Lady Jane Grey. Book
with a ruff.

Medieval tiled-floor book. The fastening was made to represent a chatelaine's girdle.

# Pulling a wax piece together

Learning new techniques and then using them in your artwork is great fun, but time spent researching, going into greater depth and incorporating these techniques is not only satisfying but rewarding too. Photography in locations, research in books, sketching, making samples and experimenting with mixed-media techniques will ultimately result in unique designs.

Sometimes it can be difficult to 'pull a piece together' when you have multiple layers. Here are a few tricks that can be used to help integrate the various elements of the piece.

- A can of webbing spray can change the appearance of your work. Spray outside and protect the ground, since the spaghetti-like spray has a will of its own. Place your work on the ground and stand well back. Do not hold the can near the work as you want a hint of marbling, not a splodge of paint. I particularly like to use black webbing spray for this simple technique.
- Attractive fusible webbing can also help to integrate a piece. It can be bought in black or white. The white variety can be painted when it has been bonded. The products Misty Fuse and FuseFX are both cobweb-like in appearance. Place the webbing over your work, cover with baking parchment and iron it into position. Prolonged, intense heat will change its appearance, so you need to watch it carefully as you iron and stop when you have the effect that you want.
- Sometimes the colours in your artwork may not gel. If you have a shiny surface, you can overcome this problem by sponging one of the Adirondack Alcohol Inks over the whole of the surface. These inks are translucent but since you are using an experimental approach, you may want to have the 'blending solution' that is also sold to go with these inks at hand, to knock back the colour a little. Use cotton wadding to apply the ink and keep it for further use, as it can be reactivated with the blending solution. The reactivated version will not be as concentrated as the original, but it can be used on other projects that require paler colours.
- Using embossing powders over stitches needs consideration as most of them will obliterate the stitch. However, used sparingly they can give a different appearance. The embossing powder used to represent the grout between the tiles on the book cover opposite resembles chalk. Heat-fixable paint was used sparingly so that the powder did not obliterate the stitches when it was activated with the heat gun.

# Perfect Paint

Perfec Paint by Earth Safe looks like and works like gesso. The difference is that it can be used on many different surfaces. The beauty of it is, that if it is sanded, it will not peel or scratch and this means that if you paint on top and then sand the surface, the white primer will remain where it is sanded and the paint will distress.

### Paint and Scrub

This technique is worked over a textured ground using Old World Peasant paint or gesso, and if you experiment you may find it works over some primers and texture mediums too.

- Apply Old World Peasant paint or gesso over textured paper and leave to dry.
- Paint over the dry surface with colour. For the background paper used for the illustration of Bess, shown below, I used Colorant from Earth Safe in Raw Sienna and Mexican Clay but the technique also works, to differing degrees, with other paints and colouring mediums. Again, leave this to dry.
- Now lightly sand the surface to distress it. The layers of colour on the raised surfaces will be sanded away to reveal the white layer underneath. Keep sanding until you have the effect you want.

Left: Bess. Copper relief foil painted with Old World Peasant paint and gesso prior to being inkjet printed. Right: Jane. Book on a hat.

### Pastel crayons

Old World Peasant paint also works with other colouring mediums. I tried it with pastel crayons and the results can be seen below. Study and think Turner. You won't end up with a Turner masterpiece, but you should achieve a blended background without muddying the colours. Inspired by Jane Austen, Turner and early 19th-century hats, the fabric for this book on a hat was made as follows:

- I used silk paper bonded with one part acrylic gloss medium to four parts water as I wanted a very strong fabric that would not tear under pressure.
- This strong paper was painted with Old World Peasant paint.
- When it was dry, pastel crayons were rubbed across the paper.
- The crayons were partially blended with a rubber. Don't overdo the rubbing or the colours will become muddy.
- Ormoline was painted over the pastels. Acrylic wax can be used instead of the Ormoline. Painting these mediums over the crayon tends to darken and blend the colours.
- When this was dry the paper was sanded to distress it.

## Combining stamps with the distressed background

The paint-and-scrub technique works well for backgrounds. Stamping with an ink pad on top of the distressed background can produce an ethereal quality as the distressed background will show through.

- Try using Old World Peasant paint as a base coat on the paper or fabric of your choice. Mulberry paper was used in the book shown below left.
- When it is dry, apply paint or pastel crayon. If using crayons seal it with acrylic wax or Ormoline. Pastel crayons were used for the book below.
- Scrunch the paper or fabric to obtain creases.
- Use a sanding block to distress the surface.
- Use a stamp to stamp on top. The ibex stamp used for the book cover below was made from Funky Foam. The distressed background shows through the stamped images.
- Use 505 glue spray to bond the paper or fabric to lightweight Vilene (Pellon) and stitch into it.

Below: Ibex on a Spanish Rock Face (left). Made with mulberry paper. Earth Tones (right). Made with silk paper.
Right: Rock Face. Cocoon-stripping paper with the paint-and-scrub technique and distressed Tyvek.

# Using Grungeboard

Grungeboard, made by Ranger, is made from compressed paper but it resembles a rubber-like lino tile. It can be bought plain or textured; the plain variety has been used here. It can be cut into shapes that can be appliquéd to fabric or it can be used as a rigid backing board, as illustrated opposite and on the following pages. It is robust, takes paint well and can be textured. As it is quite thick, it does not require a backing board. It can be machine or hand stitched. Holes should be pricked into it with a sharp needle; the use of a thimble is recommended.

Books made with Grungeboard covers can be folded to retain a spine. They do, however, require a fastening of some description in order to keep them completely closed. Alternatively, two separate covers for the back and front could be made and attached to a book block so that the book has an open embroidered spine.

As Grungeboard is so sturdy it can be used for free-standing concertina books. Try hinging boards that have been cut to size with masking tape and cover the boards and hinges with designs of your choice.

You can work directly on top of Grungeboard, as illustrated opposite.
- First decorate your board. I cut out six leaf shapes from freezer paper and ironed them onto the plain side of an A5 sheet of Grungeboard. These shapes were used to act as a resist.
- I sprayed over the entire board with Glimmer Mist spray.
- When the paint was dry, the shapes were removed and another six freezer-paper leaf shapes were ironed in different positions on the Grungeboard. Some of the shapes overlapped the first layer (see the picture, right).
- The board was sprayed again, using a different colour.
- When it was dry, the freezer-paper shapes were removed.
- Now you can add stitch and other decorative elements of your choice. I first machine-stitched and then hand-stitched the board using variegated fine silk. Finally I applied beaded Translucent Liquid Sculpey leaf shapes to the spine.

The Grungeboard with leaf shapes ironed on and overlapped.

Autumn Leaves book. The card book block was
inserted and glued to the inside cover.

# Grungeboard and wax

As Grungeboard can withstand heat, it can also be embossed or decorated using encaustic wax. The book with the leaf design opposite was coloured with encaustic waxes.

- Select a leaf that has a definite shape to it.
- Place a sheet of baking parchment on the ironing board.
- Place the leaf or leaves on the baking parchment. Iron the encaustic wax over them.
- Place the Grungeboard on a clean piece of baking parchment.
- Lift the leaves up one at a time and gently place them in position on the Grungeboard.
- Cover the Grungeboard with baking parchment.
- Use a clean iron and iron over the baking parchment to melt the wax on the leaves and transfer the pattern.
- Remove the leaves and baking parchment.
- You could paint the background with paints of your choice. For the waxed leaf book opposite the background was painted with encaustic wax. To do this, melt a different-coloured stick of encaustic wax on the iron. If you are able to, it is easier to lay the iron on a flat base without the handle. The wax will then stay in a pool on the iron as opposed to running down it. Use a designated paintbrush to paint the wax in the spaces. You will need to work quickly before the wax hardens on the bristles. (When you want to re-use a paintbrush for this technique the wax remaining on the bristles will be hard. To make it useable you will need to hold it on a clean area of the iron to re-melt the wax. Clean the brush on a piece of kitchen towel while the wax is still warm. Your brush will now be ready to paint using a different coloured wax.)
- Free machine stitch into the piece.
  **Optional:** use a thick thread to hand stitch selected areas.
- Use a paper towel to liberally apply beeswax polish to the Grungeboard.
- Use clean towels to keep rubbing and buffing until the paper towel comes away clean.
- Use encaustic wax of your choice to iron over the piece. Silver wax was used here. The wax will glide over the polished surface.
  **Optional:** apply beeswax polish again and rub and buff.

# Textured waxed Grungeboard

As Grungeboard is rigid, it can be textured with DecoArt Paper Perfect, Golden Fiber Paste or Golden Light Molding Paste. It can also be textured with stitches, as described here.

**Method**
- Machine stitch the Grungeboard.
- Iron encaustic wax over the Grungeboard and the stitches.
- Polish the Grungeboard with beeswax polish.
- Add any decorative features to the sides and spine.
- Bend the Grungeboard over a prepared book block.
- Use PVA (white craft glue) to bond the endpapers to the Grungeboard.

The covers of these books are made from Grungeboard decorated with wax. The yellow book was machine stitched before the wax was applied.

# Bookbinders' tissue and Grungeboard

Thin papers and fabrics can be used to cover the boards, and these can still be stitched into. The covers for the book below were made by placing the tissue over a textured rubbing plate. The design was transferred to the paper by rubbing a Markal Paintstik over it. When it was dry, the background was painted and then sealed, and strengthened with acrylic wax. The tissue was bonded to Grungeboard using 505 glue. Free machine embroidery was used to stitch through the layers. A second coat of acrylic wax was painted over the stitches and board to integrate the piece.

Patterned tissue on Grungeboard.

Jumping the Wake. Tyvek and silk paper on
Grungeboard. The 'wake' was formed by
bending Grungeboard and attaching it to a
flat grey board base.

# Using pulp papers

Pulp papers can be textured while they are still wet. Pressing something that has raised detail into the sheet of wet pulp will not work; the pulp needs to be hammered to obtain any texture or pattern. Texture hammers are available, but a household hammer, used on top of something textured, will also work.

As this is a messy technique I work outside or over a sink.

- Place an A4 sheet of pulp paper or Lokta pulp paper on a board.
- Pour water over the board to saturate the paper. Drain off any excess.
- Use a Tim Holtz texture hammer to give texture to the paper, or place something with raised detail over the paper and hammer on top of it.
- Leave the paper to dry.
- Colour the paper and then stitch into it. The paper can be bonded to cotton wadding or lightweight Vilene (Pellon) or it can be stitched into as it is.

Below and right: Textured Lokta pulp-paper books based on a study of volcanic action and residues.

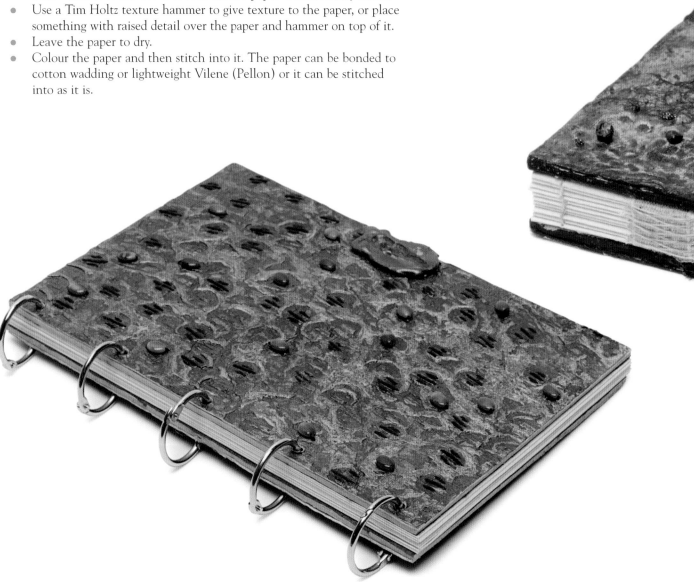

# Suppliers

**Ario**
5 Pengry Road
Loughor, Swansea SA4 6PH
01792 529 092
www.ario.co.uk
email: Fiona@ario.co.uk
*Tim Holtz products, Stewart Gill products, Jacquard computer-printable fabrics, Lokta pulp paper, Golden Digital Ground, Earth Safe products, Golden products*

**Art Van Go**
1 Stevenage Road
Knebworth
Hertfordshire SG3 6AN
01438 814 946
www.artvango.co.uk
email: art@artvango.co.uk
*Acrylic wax, Softsculpt, kozo bark, mulberry papers, InkAid, lightweight Vilene (Pellon)*

**The Paper Mill Shop**
Mainline Industrial Estate
Crooklands Road
Milnthorpe
Cumbria LA7 7LR
01539 564 951
www.thepapermillshop.com
email: info@thepapermillshop.com
*Card, speciality papers, ring binders, brads, bone folders, awls*

**Flutterby Crafts Ltd**
The Barns
Lower Henwick Farm
Thatcham
Berkshire
RG18 3AP
01635 860 900
www.flutterbycrafts.co.uk
*UK supplier of Jo Sonja's products*

**Gallery Textiles**
4a Canalside
Metal and Ores industrial estate
Hanbury Road B409
Stoke Prior, Bromsgrove,
Worcestershire B60 4JZ
01527 882 288
www.gallerytextiles.co.uk
email: info@gallerytextiles.co.uk
*Evolon fabric, Golden Digital Ground*

**Isobel Hall**
email: isobelhall@gmail.com
*Tea-bag paper, encaustic wax*

**LB Crafts**
6 Rose Court
Market Place
Olney, Buckinghamshire
MK46 4BY
01234 714 848
www.lbcrafts.com
email: shop@lbcrafts.com
*Earth Safe products*

**Nid-Noi**
126 Norwich Drive
Brighton BN2 4LL
01273 698112
www.nid-noi.com
email: info@nid-noi.com
*Evolon fabric, Lutradur*

**OCG Arts**
Market Place
Ambleside
Cumbria LA22 9BU
01539 432 022
www.ocg-arts.com
email: Sylvia@ocg-arts.com
*Silk wrapping paper*

**Oliver Twists**
22 Phoenix Road
Crowther, Washington
Tyne and Wear NE38 0AD
0191 416 6016
jean@olivertwists.freeserve.co.uk
*Degummed silk filament, cocoon strippings*

**Pfaff Embellisher machines**
VSM UK Ltd
Ravensbank House
Ravensbank Drive
Redditch, Worcestershire
B98 9NA
01527 519 480
www.pfaff.com
email: uk.info@pfaff.com
*Embellisher needle-felting machines*

**Shepherds Bookbinders**
76 Rochester Row
London SW1P IJU
020 7620 0060
www.bookbinding.co.uk
email: info@bookbinding.co.uk
*Awls, bone folders, Japanese screw punch, ring binders, screw posts*

**Texere Yarns**
College Road
Barkerend Road
Bradford BD1 4 AV
01274 722 191
www.texere.co.uk
email: info@texere.co.uk
*Cocoon strippings, silk fibres*

**21st Century Yarns**
Unit 18, Langston Priory
Kingham
Oxfordshire OX7 6UP
01608 683 762
www.21stcenturyyarns.com
email: info@21stcenturyyarns.com
*Silk yarns, embellishing packs*

# Further reading

Grafton, Carol Belanger, *Illuminated Initials*. Dover, 1995

Grey, Maggie, *From Image to Stitch*. Batsford, 2008

Hall, Isobel, *Bags with Paper and Stitch*. Batsford, 2007

La Plantz, Shereen, *Cover to Cover*. Lark, 1998

McCallum, Graham Leslie, *4000 Animal, Bird and Fish motifs*. Batsford, 2005

Smith, Sheila, *Embellish, Stitch, Felt*. Batsford, 2008

Sussman, Pam, *Fabric Art Journals*. Quarry, 2005

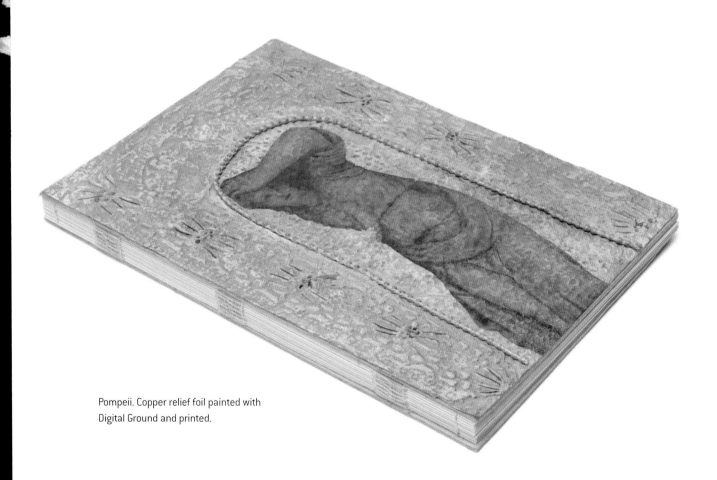

Pompeii. Copper relief foil painted with
Digital Ground and printed.

# Index